GETTING OVER VIVIAN

Jill Carstens

OPEN
BOOKS

Published by Open Books

This book is for my son and my first family: Mom, Dad and Kyle. If our life at Vivian hadn't been so wonderful, it wouldn't have hurt so much to lose it.

"The further away a story, the more clearly you can see it…
because only then can you see yourself."

—Sandra Cisneros, *A House of My Own*

PROLOGUE

February 2022

I am a statue. Not a pretty one. Mouth agape, arms sagging limp at my sides in dejection. A dark cloud returns over my head. No words enter my mind. I am so stricken by the empty space before me, like the unexpected gap in a child's smile after they lose a tooth. I just stand there, incredulous.

Twenty-Sixth Avenue. I have driven down this road my whole life; this artery that connected my childhood home, like an umbilical cord, its length stretching as I explored outside the confines of suburbia. "Twenty sixth will take you anywhere you need to go, Jill. Straight to downtown," Dad would tell me when I was learning to drive.

This spot. This spot with the hole was one of the first places I remember from our jaunts out of the neighborhood as a young family. I was barely five years old and the landscape of my mind was just being mapped out. It was one of Dad's culinary finds: A simple Mexican food place housed in a large but welcoming Victorian situated where Twenty-Sixth Avenue begins to curve, just east of Federal Boulevard, where around the hill the full glory of downtown Denver is exposed from up on the Highlands. I could get there blindfolded.

It was called La Loma. "The Hill."

The hill has been flattened, as well as that old house. Where there is a hole now.

Where is the restaurant? It is dead. This is its grave?

We came here as a family. Sometimes with Gramma or friends visiting Colorado. The grown-ups would have margaritas. The kids would watch the ladies making the tortillas. The Bronco game seemed to be always playing in the background.

It was one of our places. And now it is gone.

So many places are gone. Stolen with too much money that persuades even the most devout, loyal, long-running family business to conjure visions of endless days somewhere on a beach. Money that taunts people into retirement. But the larger, longer lasting result is that this money also transforms a neighborhood and its community. It decimates it.

I can't really take much more of this. It has become so common that I wonder if I am desensitized to the telltale chain link fences that increasingly surround my favorite places, indicating imminent demolition. For most of my life, I have known this town like my own freckles.

But now this happens. I drive to a place and it has vanished. Or I am in the process of driving only to find myself lost on a corner that has been manipulated from the landscape I've known to a concrete canyon of crappily constructed high-rises meant to contain the temporary transplants to our town.

And this latest discovery is almost causing a breakdown. I feel like falling to my knees, not just in sorrow, but also in rage. Who the hell do they think they are? Do they even know the neighborhood? Do they live in Denver? And if they do, how dare they?! Can you take claim to a view, the air? Can a person really have the power to mow down a hill?

I want to claw at the dirt that is the residue of this murder-by-bulldozer.

Now I know that I should take pictures of all of my favorite places, document them, because someday they will unexpectedly evaporate into the thin Colorado air. And as these places vanish, so do parts of me.

A Fresh Start

1968

"It snows there, but it's not as cold and the sun shines all the time. And you don't have to worry about tornadoes anymore, the Rocky Mountains will protect us."

My dad had a wonderful knack for including me in adult discussions, and as a persuasive salesman, could have convinced me of just about anything. I had survived my toddler years running to the basement of our Kansas home during tornado warnings, visions of Dorothy's uprooted home running through my mind.

My brother had just been born and I was approaching age four, a time when whatever my parents said or did, I adored them. My father's promotion of our move to Colorado, courtesy of his new job, did not disappoint. Soon I was walking our empty lot, up on a knoll on Vivian Street, with a sweeping view of those Rockies, my new best friends, protecting us from tornadoes and providing a new source of exploration.

We had our blank sheet of paper in that property, ready to fill it up with the story of our life.

Our new life that seemed as fresh as the snow that blanketed it the day they broke ground. Our house manifested out of that field, constructed by a local man named Forrest. We visited the site weekly; a wonderful evolving skeleton of timbers that slowly began forming rooms and staircases. I can still smell the fresh-cut two by fours.

The construction of our house did not happen swiftly like tract homes, where a battalion of tanned, tool-belted men swarm an area with particle boards—erecting dwellings, it seems, from directions out of a Lego box. Our house had a solid frame and bricks chosen for their character as much as for their strength.

This would be our house. My house. I grew as it grew. And so did our family. Vivian would serve as the setting, the home base, for our future experiences and the chronicling of our own history. The pouring of that concrete foundation established a passion, deep in my core, of the importance of place.

A place that becomes special because you somehow already feel a part of it. Not just the house, but the surrounding area of houses, sidewalks, trees, shrubs and sky.

Where you feel most comfortably yourself. Home.

That passion makes it all the more difficult to accept the frustrating reality that one event can demolish it all, obliterating the past as if it never existed. The child within me denying, repeatedly, over time, the harsh reality that even if I had Dorothy's magic ruby slippers, I could not bring back those mythical days.

VIVIAN

The empty fields surrounding our new home became my personal sanctuary and my first school of nature. I wandered through tall wheat-like weeds that became my own tiny forest, rich with the imagery of a young child. Our childless older neighbors helped me learn the names, seasons and color tones of the sturdy native plants of my arid surroundings—the various greens of sage, cacti and grasses, the corn-yellow of sunflowers.

Sometimes I had the privilege of witnessing the rare and brief bloom of a yucca plant, white against the blue-bird day. In the winter these plants would not disappear, but freeze like statues into faded and brittle sepia tones of their former selves until the next spring.

The world seemed my queendom then. I embraced my surroundings by stubbornly marching around barefooted, risking stepping on a random, thorn-like goat head within the dry soft dirt underfoot. I frequently ran home for a Band-Aid after stubbing my toe on the sunbaked concrete sidewalks of the neighborhood, but it seems I wouldn't have had it any other way. I was enjoying that intense sensory experience, typical in young children and craved before our brains catch up with our bodies. I connected viscerally to my environment. I especially loved squishing my toes in that dirt of those empty lots after it turned to mud from a rapidly melted spring snow.

That is something that perplexed folks from elsewhere. It is very sunny here. *Most* of the time.

My norm was playing coatless in the snow. Skiing in my shorts, under a penetrating sun, a mile up in the air. My lungs were weaned on altitude, so much so that now if I am in a humid location, rather than feel relief I am stymied, strangled by air. The Colorado climate became my religion, a baptism by sun, stunning natural beauty and high elevation. A standard by which other places would eventually be ruthlessly compared.

Home Base

Magpies argue in the ponderosa pines just outside my window as darkness transitions to bright orange beneath my eyelids. The sun seems to rise directly into my room. It's today! And this solar miracle signals to me, "What will you do? What is your great idea for today?"

My feet land on the rough, pea-green shag carpeting and I carefully tiptoe myself down the hallway, past my parents' and brother's rooms. I am the early riser and I revel in the brief solitude. I descend the staircase like a mountain climber rappelling down a wall of rock, leaping multiple steps then sliding along the railing, catching a bit of air on the last steps while holding the curli-cue end of the banister and landing in a 180 switchback onto the cold tile floor of the front entryway. Continuing along another hallway towards the kitchen, my fingers lightly skim the raised velvet design on the wallpaper—a forbidden act.

Otherwise, the interior walls of our house are painted mostly white. The large, many-paned windows, the eyes of Vivian, let in all of the sun's glory, especially in the morning, evoking a heaven-like brightness that summons me.

Our kitchen is a contrast of dark wood tones, white countertops and red accents. My parents are united in an awareness of aesthetics, intentionally demonstrated in the house's décor. We even have a red sink! Although

Dad's company was the source of most of the furnishings at Vivian, the rest of the furniture appeared courtesy of Mom's savvy with second hand pieces. Our kitchen table chairs are painted a red to match the sink and wallpaper. It is a cheerful place to wake up.

The stained glass light fixture over our kitchen table casts a reflection of us in the panes of the bay window at night during dinnertime. When I struggle to eat my soggy green beans I make faces at myself, or at my brother, who sat opposite me. My father finishes with his meal before I barely begin, sopping up his A-1 sauce with his last bite of meat, then holding his fork out like a claw ready to pounce on whatever bits we are not ingesting.

My father liked to grill out on the back porch adjacent to our kitchen in ALL weather, even in snowstorms, cigarette going, Scotch in one hand and tongs in the other. Even through my vegetarian years, the smell of steak cooking on a grill, especially on a *snowy* day, gives me a cozy feeling.

In the kitchen, the large bay window frames my two mountains—North and South Table Mesa, named for their flat, table-like summits. I pour myself a bowl of Captain Crunch, surveying those mountains, imagining a giant eating his own breakfast, using one of the mesas as his table.

Through that window, as our time unfolds at Vivian, we will be amazed by fire-in-the-sky sunsets that paint the clouds fluorescent versions of pink, purple, orange, and red. Many mornings a sunrise will reflect onto the mesas, coloring them a fantastic magenta. Over time, those two mountains become part of my family.

When I am grown, I will stand at the top of these preludes to the Rockies during a mountain bike ride and take stock of my place. My home. I take hold of it up there. Re-claim it. It remains through all of the changes. I can see the entirety of the map of my life at the edge of South Table Mesa; the house on Vivian, my personal compass, up on the knoll, then going east from there into Denver. The artery of Twenty-Sixth Avenue traces a line stretching exactly the expanse of the geography of my existence, from tabletop downhill to the valley of the city! I can see it all up there, from a mountain that greeted me every day through that big kitchen window.

Soon the rest of the family emerges from upstairs and we begin our day. My brother, often carrying his pillow and stuffed tiger, settles on the carpet directly in front of the TV as mother solicits what he might want for breakfast. Dad will reach for coffee and the paper while I might continue to contemplate what my bright idea will be.

Our family room is a favorite dwelling place. At the time, its vaulted, barn-like ceiling was a novelty. It was also the only house in the neighborhood with an open floor plan. My brother and I could consume our TV dinners at the kitchen counter while craning our necks towards the television! Despite the openness it was a cozy room with wood paneling and a fireplace flanked by bookshelves. When no one was watching, my brother and I scaled these built-in bookshelves, reaching our arms up to touch the ceiling beams, just because.

Otherwise the television is the centerpiece of this room, the big cabinet-style model that sat in a stately fashion on the floor. Our Siamese cat claimed its surface for naps warmed by the electrons of the cathode-ray tube. Rather than a remote, my brother and I are the "channel changers" for the five stations that were available in the 1970s.

When we aren't gathered together watching *The Brady Bunch* or *The Carol Burnett Show*, Kyle and I take over that room, building forts with the cushions of the couch, wrestling, play-acting or fighting over what channel to watch.

Weekends and summer days are most often

schedule-less and my brother and I have opportunities to guide the activity, which sharpens my imagination with many "maybes." Maybe I will build a house for my dolls out of the cardboard boxes in the garage. Maybe I will paint. Maybe I will get my brother to play act with me. Whatever I decide, there is rarely any push-back from my mother. She encourages our free play and doesn't seem to mind our messes.

Especially if it is a weekend, my brother and I might never get around to changing out of our pajamas, but find ourselves raiding our parents' closet to find costumes for our impromptu play.

———————

When I look in the mirror, sometimes I see her. That happy, well-taken-care-of little girl. In the upstairs bathroom of Vivian with the pink-and-orange striped wallpaper, look-ing in the mirror and wondering who I will become. Will I have a career? Will I be pretty? Will I be happy?

She is the same girl who looked in this mirror when standing on a stool to brush her teeth, right next to her little brother. Peering curiously at herself after getting glasses at age nine. The very same girl who had to get a shag haircut after her long locks got tangled inescapably in the rope of the tire swing. The pre-teen who mouthed her favorite songs into her comb, pretending to be Stevie Nicks. The one who, at that awkward age of life, had to get braces and felt ugly. And finally, the sixteen-year-old who gazes desperately at her image, in the only home she has ever really known, one last time in disbelief at the uncertainty of her future.

We had an intimacy with our home, with Vivian. How could I possibly fathom its rooms...empty? Our identity dwelled within these walls that I had watched evolve from the vacant field. The contents of our house were products of our life, *proof* of life containing emotional value. How could these items be divided? Would they be? Or would my mother or father, out of spite, impulsively dispose of our collective past in order to pretend it didn't happen? What would Vivian be without my father sipping coffee in his yellow terry-cloth robe? Without my brother staked out on the green carpet sitting too close to the television? Without my mother toiling in the kitchen? And me peacefully self-sequestered in my room, watching the world go by from my window seat?

Excursions;
Beyond Vivian Street

Click clack, click clack, my mom's heels sound on the entryway of Vivian. She calls up the stairs. "Cosmos! We're ready!"

Mom is using Dad's nickname, Cosmos. His long-time friend and co-worker, George, bestowed this name on Dad well before my birth. This term alludes to Dad's good looks and suave personality, but also his knack for evoking a *cosmopolitan* air: sophisticated, discerning, and all-around cool. This also means it takes him a long time to get ready to go out.

We hear a muffled response from Dad but know that it will still be awhile before he deems himself ready. Kyle and I are cleaned up and in our "good clothes," hair brushed and uncomfortable shiny shoes on our little feet.

We sit in the rarely-used living room adjacent to the entryway, awaiting our dad's appearance. His grooming process is a lengthy one; extensive hot shower, then, wrapped in his yellow terry cloth robe, a seat at the side table of their bedroom for a cigarette and sometimes a Scotch before using the hair dryer. I could hear the ice cube tinkle in his drink when I walked past their room earlier and the familiar scents of Dad's cologne mixed with Kool Cigarette smoke wafting out—the essences of my dad.

My brother and I, frustrated by but accustomed to our dad's routine, wiggle impatiently on the gold velvet couch. I show Kyle how to "write" in the velvet, while he takes apart the plastic grapes decorating the coffee table. Mom never seems to notice our indiscretions here. At last Dad descends the staircase, all handsome in his navy blue, gold-buttoned suit and smelling good. My mom and dad standing there together, all polished up, look like my Barbie and Ken dolls.

We all *click-clack* through the tiled entryway and out the door, *click-clacking* down the sidewalk into Dad's car. It is more than his car, it is essentially his moving office that takes him to all of his sales clients, near and far. The car is also, I have learned, an extension of my dad himself, a reflection of his success as a salesman. Thus the car must be a nice one, inside and out. Because of this, Kyle and I have strict rules about whatever we might bring into that car's backseat. Certainly never food! Or gum! The car must remain pristine!

We are headed downtown to our favorite Italian restaurant, Josephina's, in historic Larimer Square. This jaunt into the city becomes a bit of a tradition that I look forward to whenever the opportunity presents itself. We back down our hilly driveway and immediately take a soft right onto Twenty-Sixth Avenue which will take us past four major north south streets as we head east, away from the suburbs, towards downtown Denver.

My mind plays Petula Clark's tune, "Downtown" in anticipation as I watch the succession of neighborhoods parade past my view out the window. As Twenty-Sixth veers slightly downhill towards the "valley" of Denver, we enter a time warp progressing in reverse. Mom educates me on the different forms of architecture representing these time frames as we drive. From our neighborhood and the more recent homes of the 1960s and 70s to 1950s ranches with their offset angles, deco-era Craftsman brick bungalows and, finally, as we approach downtown, the ornate late 1800s Victorians, Denver's first houses. At this point in time, my city is not yet one hundred years old.

After we pass the wonderfully grungy and busy Federal Boulevard in the vicinity of Mile High Stadium, Twenty-Sixth curves to a ninety-degree angle to the north and briefly becomes Zuni Street before we turn right onto the main route of downtown, Speer Boulevard. We travel across the viaduct carrying us over the confluence of the South Platte River and Cherry Creek as the city unfolds before us. "Things will be great when you're downtown...." I get excited when I see all the city lights and tall buildings, probably influenced by the New York City montage from the show *That Girl*.

At the other side of the viaduct sits Larimer Street where Denver City was born. The buildings on this block have been lovingly preserved. After parking we wander this block where once a General William Larimer plotted the first streets and built his own residence with doors made resourcefully from coffins. Larimer Street was Denver's first main street, encompassing its first bookstore, post office, dry goods and barbershop. I marvel at the unique character and history of these turn-of-the-century buildings.

Perhaps my psyche was influenced by the event of watching Vivian evolve from the open field or my parents' attention to design and architecture, but I am affected by those details. I notice whether they are there, or not. I develop a radar for the efforts made to enhance the aesthetics of a place.

Walking Larimer as a family, I notice the ornate and diverse details of these older structures. Most notable to me is the heft of those doors; heavy and substantial, as if saying "We're here to stay!"

Josephina's entryway greets patrons with one of those

old doors, with an etched window and brass door handle. It creaks wonderfully as we enter, our noses tuned to the appetizing aromas of the Italian food. From this time on, an old creaking door will forever signal to me: this place is timeworn, containing treasures from the past, pay attention! The interior is true to the period, tin ceiling, an historic carved wooden bar, and velvet pink and red upholstered chairs. The Rat-Pack croons some familiar tunes as we survey our menus. Rarely do we stray from our usual order—a decadent deep-dish pizza loaded with meats and cheeses.

I learned later in my life that not all of my peers went on outings like this with their parents. My dad especially had the goal of sharing experiences with us. He had grown up in a very small town in rural Nebraska, knowing little outside of that town until he moved away to go to college. Dad wanted us to have an earlier start in getting to know the greater world. We sense the specialness attached to being included on these excursions. This is how the range of my geo-biography began to extend from Vivian Street to include the heart of Denver and how I claimed my city through these events.

MOM

"Is," "the," "I," "on," flash before my eyes, handwritten in black magic marker on rectangular cards my mother has prepared out of poster board. She is saying the sight word as she holds them before me, propelling me into the written word. Mom is engaging me in a program she read about in a magazine, "Helping Your Baby to Read."

I am only eighteen months old, but she and Dad see my potential. She reprints the entire Dr. Seuss book *Hop on Pop* and then we read it over and over again. I read this whole book before the age of two, catapulting me into the world of language and books which will sustain me as a lifelong reader and writer.

She took the time to read to us individually every night. The illustrations of various Golden Books are so a part of my memory that when I rediscover these books later in life it is like finding forgotten family photos. I have many Robert Louis Stevenson poems memorized from when she read *A Child's Garden of Verses* and Winnie the Pooh's outlook on life still resonates with me, narrated in my head by my young mother's voice.

My still chubby five-year-old hands are awkward with the skinny, water-soaked paint brush as I swirl it into the orange pallet of my watercolor set. Why does everything turn to brown on my paper? Frustrating! I eventually give up on watercolors and stick with tempera paint and by fifth grade I graduate to real acrylics. As much as riding my bike and writing in my journal will become faithful modes of release for me, dipping my brush into a thick blob of colorful paint will become the only activity that allows my busy brain a break. It all starts at the round kitchen table in front of the bay window on Vivian Street where Mom supports my messy endeavors with all things *art*.

My communication and emotional abilities develop at that kitchen table too, under the stained glass light fixture as I vent to Mom about my troubles with friends at school. She is a good listener and never really tells me what to do, just listens.

In the summers she sends me to art classes and we visit the museums so often that the buildings and many of their permanent exhibits remain a cherished part of the pages in the mental maps of my personal history.

While I explore art, my brother designs structures with his Legos in front of our television or locks himself in the bathroom to concoct potions in the sink with soap, toothpaste and other cleaning products. His experimental nature often travels over to the kitchen where he freely investigates ingredients, preparing diverse snacks, like ketchup and mustard mixed together forming an orange paste into which he would dip potato chips. He has a *unique* palette, eating Elvis-inspired sandwiches made from combinations like peanut butter and mayonnaise— all of this activity foreshadowing his eventual occupation. While I endeavor to steal cookies from the cookie jar, my mother participates in his salty preferences as they make Velveeta and catsup tostadas under the broiler or share a jar of pickles.

Our individual and collaborative activities at Vivian evoke a productive hum in the house, each of us immersed in some sort of joyous project.

Who is that pretty blond woman sitting at the petite

kitchen desk, telephone positioned under her chin and phonebook cradled in her arms like a newborn? That's my mom! Mom, or "Jude," as my dad calls her, spent a lot of time on the phone calling citizens to inform them of upcoming ballot issues. Not your average housewife, Mom had selfless intentions towards civic duty.

Household chores are not her favorite, but Mom is in no way apathetic. Many hours are spent on tasks of volunteer service. Tethered to the kitchen phone for hours, she almost wears out her dialing finger educating citizens about various community reforms.

Kyle and I spent reluctant summer days walking door to door with her, clipboard in hand, seeking to register people to vote. The smell of coffee and crayons forever reminds me of the Sunday school room in a church where once a month Mom met with the Lakewood Chapter of the League of Women Voters.

Later in life I would unearth a yellowed brochure from 1972, put together by the organization "Plan Jeffco." My mother was an active member. Their efforts saved most of my foothills, like South Table Mesa, from development by creating Jeffco Open Space.

Sometimes Mom needs to attend meetings at night. She heads to the garage door, all lipsticked-up with an armful of manila folders. Kyle predictably cries disturbing the unlikely babysitter—Dad—who is relaxing in his recliner. I wail at her, "WHY do you have to go to *another* meeting?!"

One time, instead of blowing kisses and escaping quickly out the garage door, Mom bent down to my eye level. I could smell her perfume and hairspray as she gave me a serious look and informed me that her meeting was about fighting air pollution. Ever since the commercial with the crying Indian, my active young brain has been preoccupied with solving the pollution dilemma. I even drew pictures of inventions to correct this problem—it was a big concern to me. When Mom told me she was essentially going to help fix Denver's "brown cloud," my complaints were immediately silenced. I try not to protest about her meetings anymore and set about helping to calm my baby brother.

DAD

"I think I heard him over in the next aisle!" Like an auditory scavenger hunt, my brother and I run towards my dad's distinctive smoker's cough. We are on a rare trip to the grocery store with Dad in the evening when the store is relatively empty. My brother and I relish the chance to run unsupervised through the wide and polished aisles. Dad rarely goes to the grocery store and he gets distracted. One moment he is asking us to find the peanut butter, the next he has disappeared.

Mom tackles trips to the grocery store with a detailed list organized by aisle, Dad *wanders, browses*. The only time he might take this trip is when he is out of cigarettes or some other "Dad-necessity." Otherwise, when Dad contributes to the shopping it usually means we're having company. And company necessitates "fancy food." He will emerge from an aisle with products Kyle and I have never seen: water chestnuts, Liquid Smoke, delicacies from the deli... It is indeed more of an adventure when we accompany Dad to the store.

"There you are!" I exclaim exasperated, "You know, Dad, you're not supposed to *leave* us, that's not the way Mom does it!" He offers me a look of mock shame, combined with a wry smile, suggesting, "But my way is more fun!"

Raised by his aunts on a farm in rural Nebraska, "food was food!" he will remark when he reminisces on being spoiled with after-school treats of Hershey Bars and Lays potato chips. But by contrast, he witnessed those eccentric aunts preserving food they'd grown on-site. Dad grew up intrinsically aware of scarcity. The foreboding possibility of poverty can manifest into strength and resourcefulness for some people. My dad came to realize the rewards of hard work and what money could do to change a tough situation.

He was not originally a good student, in fact, he says the teachers labeled him as "stupid." It is a wonder that he had the courage to continue on and put himself through college. When participating in football prevented him from achieving good grades, he quit. He became the dorm RA, worked a job in the cafeteria and studied late into the night in the library. He turned his grades around and got himself a sales job upon earning his BA, with my mom on his arm.

While Mom had grown up with post-war suburban security, translating for us a fairly laid-back parent, Dad's childhood experiences converted to high expectations. He wanted us to thrive, never to experience the circumstances that he'd had. I was fascinated by this very different life my dad had before becoming my dad.

I scoured the precious few black-and-white photos of his family that Mom had arranged in an album. Dad had been poor! Photos depicted desolate fields and run-down buildings of the family farm with the stoic looks of his long-gone, German-born relatives, conveyed with such distinction in colorless form. These images were so different from the bright and happy Coca-Cola fueled, colorful Polaroids of my own childhood and have always given me instant respect for his origins and how he became who he is.

What makes some people seem innately determined to escape such challenges, while others wallow in them? How does a person transition out of a difficult situation? That is a question that I have contemplated my entire life—the ability, the potential, we all *can* have to change ourselves and our destiny. Manifest a significant interruption. Create a new map for ourselves.

Partly because of my family DNA and partly inspired by my dad's ambition, I prove myself to be a good student and Dad dreams out loud about my future. We talk about some of his friends' kids, one in particular who just got into the University of Hawaii. "With good grades you could go to any school you want," he suggests proudly.

This was no small gift. My dad was not easy to impress and I craved his approval. Because school was never easy for him, I was a bit of an enigma to him. I remember one Sunday autumn afternoon happily holed-up in my room, sitting in my bean bag chair. I had a tall stack of books from the library sitting next to me when Dad peeked in. "Whacha doin'?" he asked. "Reading!" I replied, holding my book up happily. He looked at me with a bit of wonder, an expression of both pride and bewilderment at my decision to sometimes forego television or friends for a stack of books.

In A College Daze

1983

I am invisible. Invisible to myself as well to the hordes of giggling strangers, stuffed into this cracker box building, all of whom seem to have become best friends in a matter of hours. I go early to the dining hall to get my meals, avoiding crowds and the embarrassment of eating alone. I really don't care about all these silly people anyway. Silly is not part of my emotional repertoire right now.

As I hover over my desk in the dorm room, straining to stuff the senseless contents of an econ book into my head, I think to myself, "Fuck this!" Where are the ivy-covered buildings? Where are the sweater-clad intellects? I am surrounded by idiots who just want to drink beer and skip class. Classes are to be endured rather than contemplated and discussed. I hate this place. But I have nowhere else to go.

About a month ago my mother, who I feel I barely know anymore, dropped me off at the state university located an hour and a half north of Denver. That day, under the green tint of the fluorescent light in the middle of the prison-cell-like cinder block dorm room, I remember sighing deep inside, perhaps not recognizing that I was enduring a dull depression.

This was not how this chapter of my life was supposed

to go. Standing awkwardly among some boxes and a suit-case, it was clear my mom was ready to leave. Still so pretty, she has a new short hair cut for selling real estate. This change adds to all the other changes that I can't keep up with. Mom seems to also have a new serious persona, an urgency to get going to do whatever she does now. We pre-tended not to hear the enthusiastic conversations as other families down the hall helped new students get settled, hang posters, make lunch plans. My mother was ready for me to start a different life, because she already had. And we hadn't been getting along in her new life. After a barely audible murmur about birth control, she left.

And here I am sitting by myself, in this hard chair, attempting to study, just like I did the last year and a half of high school. It's all a blur now. I mostly maintained my high GPA but spent many nights completely alone in the small house Mom replaced us in, just staring down at my textbooks. I really just didn't care anymore. Mom and I fought—horrible, rage-filled, red-faced, hormone-fueled fights. All the time. My eyes were almost always red and puffy. My friends pretended not to notice.

I hardly saw my brother anymore. Mom took him along on some of her excursions with her new boyfriend. Sometimes neither of us knew where he was. He was only eleven. Where *was* he?

We saw Dad once a week, but his eyes were even redder than mine.

I was simply still stunned, mute, about what had hap-pened to my previous life. It was like not existing anymore. If everything that had reflected my sense of self was gone, how could I see myself? I couldn't—I was a hazy, foggy, half version of who I thought I had been. My former life and what I had perceived as my future was locked away in an old, yellowed home movie in a house that wasn't mine anymore. I could conjure myself and that life in my mind, but it was otherwise gone, erased from existence.

Heavy books weigh me down as I trudge among the other thousands of freshmen across the expansive stretch of lawn separating the dorms from the classrooms in the early morning chill. Through my despair I feel a pent-up resentment in the pit of my stomach. Or more accurately, a melancholy like someone had cut a hole in my soul.

The pretense of norm, fabricated by my parents' attempts at being supportive, came in the form of springing for a new college look. Indeed, we'd been an upper middle class family who had had all the "things." But I knew better now. Money certainly can't buy love. And what I missed was not a lifestyle. I missed a place in time. I missed my home, my family and my neighborhood where I knew everyone and felt a part of a community.

The preppy clothes that Dad had spent a fortune on felt more like a costume when placed on my awkward-feeling body. I could hear the salesman in him saying, "Dress to impress!" In my catatonic state, I had permitted Mom to take me to the salon where my long blond locks had been chopped into a horrible 80s new wave mullet. I flinched at my reflection in the mirror, this haircut exposing my chubby-round face. I didn't recognize myself. I didn't like myself either.

And as much as I hate the simple, characterless structures that compose this campus, the banal landscape mimics my attitude. I am in no way motivated. Otherwise, the more I perceive the deficit of intellect here the more I quietly crave it, resulting in even more feelings of resentment.

These bitter feelings lingered not only at our parents' unexpected split and loss of our home, but of letting me down here. This campus is not what I worked for all those years. I was supposed to be surrounded by inspiration. Inspiration in the environment is critical for me, I was realizing. That need had surely been cultivated by an earlier life of observation and appreciation of all things beautiful, whether it was the consistent azure of the Colorado skies and the majesty of the mountains or the unique details thoughtfully curated into the architecture of historic buildings, representing various eras of time. The architecture of an area represents the intention and integrity of its particular time period. Environment can provoke us in negative as well as positive ways.

Where was the beauty of intention here? I am surrounded by unremarkable squares and rectangles of post war; practical concrete architecture that feels like I'm meandering through a black-and-white dream. Everything looks the same. It feels like going to school at a military base. Sterile. This town is barely a rest stop off of a highway going no direction I care to go.

Back at Vivian, when I had just started high school, my parents had acted "normal," not realizing I heard their late night conversations while sneaking downstairs. I had also accidentally intercepted a phone call from our minister encouraging my dad to try to "work it out." Why were they suddenly so unhappy?

I would become confused as I observed Dad putting his arm around Mom more often, expressing endearments. He was *trying!* He even showed up one day with an expensive suede coat for Mom. They would work it out, I silently hoped.

The culminating event took place when I returned home from school one afternoon. I found my father on the back porch, weeping. Not just a few tears, he was sobbing. He stared out at freshly purchased shrubs that represented the beginnings of a long-planned landscape project he had finally started in our yard. He was constantly planning improvements for Vivian. Tears streaming down his cheeks, he blew his nose from a roll of paper towels.

In that moment I changed forever.

I was compelled to grow up all in one moment as I tried to console Dad. He was falling apart in front of me. I immediately transformed from daughter to therapist. It will take a long time to understand the ramifications of this role reversal, of trying to parent your parent.

For Dad's sake I attempted to hide my panic. This is happening. Something terrible is happening to my family. My dad, my rock, was unhinged. Now I had to try to be the rock. The subsequent dismantling of my family will cause a stretch of sustained panic. Of unrest, deer-in-the-headlights alarm, taking hold of my chest, my heart, my entire being. Life suddenly became impermanent. And the subsequent fear of losing the people and things I loved became my inevitability. It became my norm.

Soon it seems the only role my brother and I have is to stretch ourselves impossibly like tightropes, spanning the frustrating distance between our parents' new houses. Two Thanksgivings, two Christmases, two Easters? "Isn't that great?" they recite over and over.

No. It is not great. It is empty and exhausting. Two new dwellings holding separate parents does not equal more. I was beginning to understand that the whole unit of our family nestled together at Vivian was, indeed, a much greater total emotionally than its now separate parts. Kyle and I have no sense of home in those places where our parents have partnered with strangers. More equals zero for us and one day that tightrope is going to snap.

From that moment on the back porch I "grew up" to try to take care of Dad. But the rest of me will take much longer to mature. The stress of care-taking and worrying about my dad overruled what should have been a more light-hearted time of my life as a teenager. In my previous life, I would have taken my time to develop, season myself as a person, found out who I was and who I wanted to be.

But here I am. At college. And even though Dad is a shadow of who he was, the encouragement he gave me back at Vivian perseveres, so I struggle to push through. What choice do I have?

I study, go to the occasional kegger, feign the false laughs and hair flips of other girls, and when I am back in Denver, resume the comfort of my relationship with my old high school boyfriend. All I want to do is to get college over with and "start my life." Lately, it was all just a big disappointment.

At the time, lost in so many ways, I was unable to verbalize how I felt. I rarely found anyone to have a substantial conversation with. I know now that I was in limbo. Because of the dismantling of my family, I did not feel that I had a home, a home base, to come home to during college breaks. I was without a compass. My map lacked any coordinates. I felt displaced physically and emotionally. I had absolutely no place where I felt grounded.

Depressed or not, the business degree my father had prescribed was not in the cards for me. At heart, I was a liberal arts gal. My mind had developed during the ideals of the late 1960s and 70s where the integrity of outdated institutions were questioned and the issues of pollution and social justice were more important than bragging about how much money you made.

While struggling with my classes, I finally summoned the courage to broach the subject of changing my major. I called Mom. She *did* know why these classes were not working for me. She had helped cultivate my creative and literary skills. She also understood that disappointing Dad was an unsavory proposition. So after having a few rare one-on-one discussions with her over the phone, like we once had at Vivian's kitchen table, I confidently made the switch to the School of Journalism. Mom still knew me and her support helped tremendously. It was a relief to enter a field of study where I felt more comfortable and with that relief, I finally warmed to the task of socializing. I leaned into my situation and surrendered.

Productions
(finding purpose and skipping class)

Holding the piece of paper my advisor gave me, I wander half-heartedly, fighting the negative feelings that had become the only constant in my life. Through the hallways of the busy student union I searched for the university events council, or "The Productions Office." I had been advised to seek some sort of internship.

I found the office hidden down a hallway I didn't know existed.

I entered, unnoticed, to a bustling office. It was a hectic place filled with animated conversations consisting of topics as diverse as the people discussing them: budgets, folding chairs, missing contracts and broken copy machines. An eclectic mix of faculty and students from all spectrums buzzed around, nerdy-looking guys in their fifth year of undergrad, sleep-deprived girls wearing Army fatigues and sporting unbrushed hair. I found a spot next to the wide-eyed freshmen sitting cradled on a burnt-orange thrift store couch. Refreshingly missing were any signs of a popped collar.

The buzz in the office had to do with a recent unprecedented booking of a series of national acts that would soon perform on campus for the first time since the early 1970s.

This all-student staff was preparing to host the recently rebooted band Chicago, who were sustaining number one hits on the Billboard Hot 100. The Productions Office was the nucleus of this venture, receiving more time, attention and money from the university and beyond than it had in decades.

The collective stress mixed with the enthusiasm was infectious. I wanted to feel that purposeful. I watched this group of people who seemed already grown up, doing all these big important tasks. I decided I wanted to be a part of this.

My journalism major helped me get accepted to the organization, and within days I feel like I've been working with this group for years. My new cohorts aren't like the kids in the dorms or fraternities. This was a rag-tag but resourceful collection of thrift-clothes-wearing, beer-chugging, class-skipping individuals intent on establishing careers in the entertainment business. They were a gritty bunch, and many had been through tough times. I didn't dare mention the source of my inner darkness which seemed insignificant compared to some of their tribulations.

As part of the Promotions Committee, I find a rhythm to my days as I write press releases and mock-up flyers for events. The work becomes extremely intuitive for me. I also begin to finally make some new friends.

Karen had been one of the wide-eyed students sitting on the couch that first day. We became fast friends while collaborating and giggling at the absurdity of editing a promotional video using two VHS players in a janitor closet down the hall from the office. I share my discovery of a new band to use as background music. While we listen I find out that she is predictably from Denver, from the southeast area where Dad now lives. It was comforting to finally know someone from a part of town that had otherwise seemed so foreign to me.

It's the first time that I have found common interests with a fellow student who wasn't more preoccupied with her appearance than the task at hand. Sometimes we are so immersed in our projects that we never go to sleep, sharing knowing smiles the next day while passing in the hallways wearing the same clothes from the day before, rumpled from a nap on that burnt-orange couch.

Was I having fun? My creative inclinations that were generated at Vivian's kitchen table had been pushed aside since the divorce and buried in SAT tests as I finished high school. I had forgotten how anything that felt creative to me was a tool for rebuilding my spirit. It made me happy.

After some of my peers mock me as a "type A" student, I surrender to skipping class on occasion to join them for beers as the Chicago concert approaches. Our mutual anxiety is tempered by the excitement for the show itself.

Two days before the band arrives a semi-truck pulls up behind the auditorium. A pirate-like, bandana-clad and steel-toed-boot-wearing bunch of roadies spill out. We all take part in unloading heavy sound equipment and then begin preparing the floor and stage. Miles of duct tape unfurl as we secure cords and thoroughfares along the lines of folding chairs on the floor. The exhaustion of this work is made less mundane as we imagine the event. Will we get to meet the band?

These fresh experiences were just the medicine I needed to shake me out of the prevalent feelings of hopelessness. Going to class, sitting among hundreds of other students in these theater-type classrooms, had not been stimulating to me. I needed more interaction and the work with Productions gave me that.

I finally had something to care about at college other than getting through it! Joining Productions unexpectedly gave me back a compass, helping guide my days, providing a much-missed sense of purpose. I was finally exploring new roads on my life-map. I ditched the preppy-student look that I never felt comfortable in, visiting the thrift stores myself. I embraced a "granola" look, we called it then: long hippie skirts, chunky sweaters, funky boots and lots of turquoise jewelry, which I still wear to this day. I also happily began growing out my "girl-mullet."

As part of a team with collective ambitions, I was feeling connected for the first time in years. By partaking in the arts again I felt more connected to me, the artistic me, who had gotten lost along the way.

The Chicago show was a huge success and led to a year full of similar experiences, permitting me introductions to many more musicians. I broadened my knowledge of music from the jazzy trumpeting of Maynard Ferguson to the bouncing new wave beats of Oingo Boingo.

As we worked and played together, for the first time in a long time I began to feel *attached* again. I developed a sense of pride in being a part of these events and the plain campus began to grow on me. I was reminded that sometimes a place is not significant until you add the people. The people mingling and *connecting* in the space of the place is vital. Parts of campus I never gave a second thought to before became endeared spots to me after I spent time in them with this group. The student union became a home away from home.

I could have foregone my college courses and worked with this group indefinitely. However, influenced by my freewheeling cohorts, some of my grades fell into the average category and skipping class began to take its toll. I was approaching my senior year of college and pressure from my father was starting to weigh me down. It was time to concentrate on what I would indeed do after graduation. I had to get back on track, work on my degree and figure out how to actually earn a living someday. Working with Productions had given me hands-on experience with marketing, so I sought to put my focus there.

Despite my hard work, by the time graduation came up in 1987, Denver was in the midst of a huge economic slump. The first layoffs were happening in the marketing departments! Full circle, it seemed, my college experience was ending as it had begun. My mood almost matched the feeling of my first days there—confusing, unpromising. The future was extremely vague...limbo once again.

Haunted By
Dad's Ambition

Dad's presence at Vivian was pervasive whether he was home or out on the road. He held court in the house. We were most often not allowed to enter his den. Whenever I did sneak into this room, I would sit at the throne of his regal wooden desk that smelled deliciously of varnish. If I picked up his telephone, I breathed in the familiar scents of my dad: Aramis cologne, Binaca breath freshener and Kool cigarettes.

"Jude, did you press my shirts?!" The whole household is on hold while Dad prepares for the annual furniture mart in Dallas. I can hear my mom reacting to his requests, scurrying down to the laundry room to iron his dress shirts. Dad was a perfectionist, but also a bit of a procrastinator. His preparations would begin the night before his flight and last well past my bedtime. Despite how much he traveled, my big strong Dad was terrified of flying and this fear would heighten his anxiety.

We didn't dare approach him during these preparations as he might snap at us. He would have everything laid out on the bed as he crossed items off of his mental list of necessities. He not only had to be dressed to the nines the entire week he was at the mart, but he also had to have all of his upholstery samples organized. Sometimes I helped with this sorting task.

As if none of that chaos had happened, Mom would wake us up early the next morning to see Dad out the door. He would be standing in the entryway with all of his luggage and heavy sample case staged all around him by the open door, ready to load the trunk. He was all calm and ready now and gave us good hugs and promises to bring something back for us. We would watch him drive off, waving him out of sight.

When Dad returned over a week later, our poodle Mitzi, always holding vigil at the front window, could hear his car coming from miles away. She would begin yelping excited shrieks as his car came into view. We'd all run to the door. "Dad's home!" What a fantastic welcome he would receive.

My understanding of Dad's job came from these experiences. I might answer phone calls at dinnertime from a woman I never met named Leslie, "Hi honey, is your daddy home?" Leslie was the owner of Kacey Fine Furniture, his biggest client. She never hesitated to call on off hours and Dad often grimaced when I reported, "It's *Leslie!*" He whispered, "Tell her I'm not home, take a message." Thus began my unofficial position as his secretary.

As I got older he also hired me to organize his invoices. This led me to know, only in my imagination, the stores and small towns he visited when he was not home. He told stories of traveling to remote towns during snowstorms in a time before the SUV. No wonder he often needed a Scotch upon returning home! In my adult life, while on a road trip, a sign on the interstate will ignite the back of my memory as one of those towns Dad traveled to: Pueblo, Montrose, North Platte, Grand Island...

Dad was ambitious and goal oriented. He liked to make plans. When we were toddlers, Mom and Dad traveled to far away beaches with their neighbor friends and a once-a-year ski trip, called The Annual, with old college friends from Nebraska. As we got older, we joined them and enjoyed trips skiing and beach-combing. Dad definitely imparted the value of home base, from which to safely embark on adventures outside of the known and comfortable realm to gain both perspective and knowledge.

Dad was a "foodie" before that was a term, and food was also part of his method for expanding our horizons. Sometimes he would return from a sales meeting bearing local culinary treats to share with us: rectangular pizza from Omaha's beloved La Casa or White Castle burgers from St. Louis, kept warm in the vinyl container he had custom-made to carry these snacks home on the plane.

STAGNANT

MTV became the only thing I had to look forward to. I would come home from my restaurant job to collapse on my dad's couch in this bland dwelling I called The Divorce House. Still wearing my uncomfortably tight polyester uniform and ugly maroon apron, I'd pop open a Diet Coke and start a frozen meal in the microwave.

As much as I usually enjoyed discussions with Dad, he'd shifted to the unpleasant recitation of statistics he read in *USA Today* regarding the overwhelming number of unemployed college graduates living at home across the nation, a big frustration to their 1950s-generation parents. Dad, ever the skilled salesman, could place an emphasis on key words like, "disappointing," "dead-end," and "unmotivated," in a way that made them seem to hover in the air like a cartoon text bubble, extending their effect. Although I had the mesmerizing, unending distraction of the latest music videos in front of me, I had way too much time to reflect on my increasingly unbearable situation, Dad's words resonating in my head.

But being unhireable was not entirely my fault. There was indeed a reason for this lack of job opportunity, the downturn in Denver's economy. The newspapers described Denver as "stagnant." Most of downtown was deserted, one third of its office buildings stood vacant.

Between where my mother and father lived

geographically, I had about ten crappy jobs the first eighteen months after college graduation. The odor of cheap Mexican food from so many of the unappetizing restaurants I worked in still makes me nauseous.

There were no jobs. Denver had been oil dependent in its workforce, the Opec Oil Crisis having its gradual and shattering effect. Our population actually decreased substantially in the 1980s. It certainly was not a great time to look for a job or start a career. In fact, it was more a time to flee, which I was just not brave enough to do yet.

THE PLAID CARPET

Today I am struggling as I attempt to unroll a forgotten, awkwardly huge piece of carpeting that my dad has stashed down here in the basement. The carpet, incredibly, still smells new even though it has been six years now since my parents' split. A split that was really like a horrible car crash with injuries, damage, PTSD.

The carpet is heavy, but I've got that maniacal energy I get when I want to be productive. It had indeed been brand new just months before my parents announced their plans to separate in that very room, the family room, at our old house on Vivian Street.

Dad had been meticulously updating our late 1960s décor. The pea green shag carpeting that my brother and I had crawled and played upon as children was replaced by this colorful plaid, low pile carpet. Our traditional furniture was switched out for sleek blue leather couches, placing the room firmly in the new decade of the 1980s.

We had spent a lot of life in that room as a family. It was the base of operations for my brother and I where the TV was on all day. We wrestled on that pea green carpet, played board games and sometimes put on shows for our parents.

Christmas was spent in that room, the tree situated right next to the fireplace. The scent of pine immersed my young senses as I fantasized about Santa and gazed at my distorted reflection in one of the green or red glass globes on the tree.

I can still smell the popcorn popping. We'd gather, all four of us, for the ABC Saturday Night Movie. Dad, sitting in his mustard-colored recliner, would instruct my brother and me when to change the channel as Mom doled out the snacks.

Why does it seem like after Dad redecorated we didn't gather as much? If he hadn't replaced the carpet, would they still be together? Should I resent this carpet?

But I am attempting to carve out a little privacy for myself to elude my father's constant judgmental gaze. So in the meantime, I am setting up an art studio in his unfinished basement. It smells a bit damp, but I don't care. Art is one of the only things that gets me to stop thinking. I toil under the dim light of one bare light bulb hanging above me, surrounded by depressingly cold and gray concrete walls.

It seems no matter what I do to feel better, I feel this dark visor-thing continually hovering just over my eyebrows. I swear I have even reached up to move it, but it is invisible.

I try to shake it off while I turn my focus back to unfurling this damn carpet. *Make something better happen, Jill!* I am going to imagine a cozier space down here. Maybe I'll find a small lamp, bring down my stereo system.

Something pops up out of the carpet. It is so small, but this tiny brick suddenly has the power to transport me, like a miniature time machine. I am paralyzed. How did I even see it? It is one of my little brother's Legos.

Even after the pea green shag carpeting was removed and this fancy new carpeting put in its place at Vivian Street, my brother could still be found sitting in front of the television building Legos after school.

This memory creates an ache deep inside me. When

visions of Vivian Street suddenly appear, they take me hostage, down a hole. The black visor, ever-present.

It is like a drug, this temptation to return to the past. Like a pendulum marking the beat of a timeless moment, I remember swinging on my swing in the backyard of Vivian, barefoot and smiling. Back and forth. Joyful. Up in the air so blue. My blond hair reflecting the sun, giggles drifting through a warm summer breeze. Childhood simplicity and innocence illuminated through this one fluid act. The to and fro motion, not unlike a cradle rocking, alternating in rhythm, blue sky, green grass, blue sky, green grass. Feeling the freedom of a bird. That time, that sunny-day setting enveloped my mind, body and spirit. Vivian was an integral part of who I had become. If only that old swing could act as a time machine that could catapult me back to that idyllic freedom layered in the security of home like a warm blanket.

Now I am willingly climbing down, slowly, rung by rung, deeper into the black hole, the sewer of my annihilated memories. But I keep going, it's too late, they have me. The memories in their broken state have been resting in a little piece of the neglected organ that is my heart. They hide here until I come to get them, even though I know it's not good for me. I descend.

I miss it so much. The house. Our things. Our family. Any sense of familiarity.

I want to run to my brother right now and hug him tight. Even though he is certainly not a little boy anymore. He is an angry young man, trying to put his life together, like me.

I hug the Lego to my chest, held tight in my fist. Even though it is sad, it is nice to hold this proof of life. All else is on pause now. I take the Lego, holding it like a precious treasure from an archeological dig, and head upstairs to my room to look for a place to keep it safe.

CHEVROIDS

Once I made my new digs inhabitable, I began creating hand painted T-shirts down in that basement studio. I wore some of them and gave some to friends. Pretty soon, friends were asking me to create customized shirts. While at my current job in the cafeteria of the Chevron building in the Tech Center, I was approached by a young corporate minion who suggested I create T-shirts for their employee baseball team. These young corporates self-deprecatingly called themselves "Chevroids" and asked me to create a logo illustrating this term.

I was thrilled at the opportunity to use my brain and creative juices. I designed a sort of stick-figure baseball player, using the Chevron logo as the body. The guys loved it and paid me in advance to make shirts for the whole team. In addition, the logo was so well received by the yuppies that it was suggested I make some extra and put them in the building's general store. I did and they started to sell.

Weeks later, I came home from work to find my father waiting behind his big old desk, glasses in hand with an angry, condescending look on his face. Previously oblivious to what I had been doing in his basement, he asked me about the T-shirts and then went off on me. "What were you thinking, messing with a corporate giant like Chevron?"

I was stumped, especially since everyone seemed to

love my T-shirts. Then Dad played back a message on his answering machine. It was a deep, self-important voice of some VP/CEO higher-up at Chevron, asserting that the logo I designed disrespected the company, violated copyright laws and that they would immediately remove and destroy the shirts. Dad indicated that I would be smarter to continue looking for a better job rather than mess around with these T-shirts in the basement. My first entrepreneurial experiment was a failure in many ways, but I was left with a tiny bit of satisfaction that I had "messed with a corporate giant!"

Cowtown
Underground

I park the car, a nice car compared to the wrecks that line this urban avenue, some missing their tires, jacked up with cinder blocks and then abandoned. I feel obvious compared to the grit that surrounds and seems to impugn me as I cautiously exit the car, me the white, middle class suburbanite. But my brother is watching for me from the porch of the ramshackle Victorian he has moved into with his friends right off of Colfax on Emerson Street.

"You found it!" He chuckles at me, the naïve person I am right now. I catch a whiff of marijuana as I enter his living room. Such luxe architecture here in Capitol Hill that, for decades, has been mostly left to fall apart. I scan the house with a mixture of envy and disgust as I practically drool at the high ceilings and an actual turret, compared with the unkempt status that is typical of young men living together.

It became an adventure to visit him, a steady string of characters—hookers, drug pushers, the homeless and patrons to the gay bar across the street—parading by as we sat on the ample porch. It was as if Kyle had moved to a third world country or a post-war territory. Many of his neighbors were destitute, on drugs, probably beating their wives, maybe a little crazy. I felt a mixture of fear and excitement, but he was thriving here.

As I floundered, I found myself seeking out any possible form of culture or authenticity to relieve my staid situation. Dad's house was situated in an area off of south I-25 near the Denver Tech Center and contained a lot of the cookie cutter, repetitive architecture that I despised, lacking any sort of character or the existence of mature trees. Although it was a long drive from Dad's house, I found myself gravitating more and more to the downtown Denver area, a midpoint between my parents' separate coordinates on my map.

Kyle eventually discovered how cheap the rent was in Capitol Hill. Capitol Hill, filled with once opulent Victorians dating to the late 1800s, was in a sad state in those days, also a victim of the bad economy, urban flight and crime. But my resourceful and rebellious brother saw the area for its character and low rent. It was dirt cheap! Banners thrown in front of buildings read "First and last month's rent *free!*" and "Free Heat!"

Kyle was taking classes downtown at Metro State. He also had ditched the idea of the business degree and was passionately pursuing photography. His neighborhood served as his muse as he documented the art of the forgotten.

Kyle had an eye. A pile of junk left in the alley was an impromptu still life. The deep wrinkles inflicted upon the homeless guy walking by with his shopping cart of belongings became as rich and tangible as a Van Gogh brush stroke, made unforgettable in Kyle's abilities with the aperture and skills in the dark room. He always clicked the shutter using black-and-white film. Yes, film. No button to push to immediately gain a sepia tone or an "enhanced" effect. Kyle spent a lot of time and money he did not really have acquiring the chemicals and paper to coax out just the right amount of light and shadows upon his subjects.

As much as our father chastised this choice of existence, I was envious of my brother's bravery to do his own thing. Kyle's life choices were the perfect antidote to our past and he did not mince words about our parents. After the divorce he had transformed abruptly, almost cruelly, from adolescence into adulthood. He felt screwed over. Rebellion was his revenge.

I grasped at my memories of a sugary sweet childhood like the delicate wisps of a dried dandelion, one breath sending them away forever. Kyle spit upon our past. Our childhood was a façade to him. A lie that was told over and over until reality came in the form of my parents' destructive decisions.

Yet, we were bonded in our feelings of abandonment. Although I chose to be sad and Kyle chose to be angry, we were the only people who understood that about each other, even if we might disagree. We were both lost on a road trip, converging at a metaphorical gas station, searching for a map, the way to go, forge ahead.

We found direction in creative endeavors. While living in Capitol Hill, Kyle started his own urban revolution with a crossover of artsy, nonconformist friends. This collection of suburban survivors comprised just a handful of young people inhabiting the inner city, dwelling within the skeletons of these old mansions and disregarded dives.

His tribe walked the streets among the vagrants, sometimes knowing them by name. They got to know the longtime owners of those diners and bars. Without realizing it, they were revitalizing the area. *Not* gentrifying it. They were creating a community within the ingredients that were already part of our city. An enclave of raw visionaries.

At some point Kyle dug out his old drum set that he hadn't touched since junior high. Suddenly he was in a band, playing at little known 3.2 bars and coffee houses and often at the now legendary Mercury Café, a haven for those few rebels. The Mercury was the epitome of "granola," not a yuppie in sight! Marilyn the owner drove an old Mercedes that ran on the used frying oil from her kitchen. She grew vegetables on the roof that subsidized all the vegetarian goodness served at the café. This place was a physical homage to the Beats, offering open mic nights for any willing poet or musician. Walking in through a velvet curtained breezeway, twinkly lights lit the eclectically decorated space. It was an oasis.

The patrons were many of Kyle's peers who had escaped college, avoided mainstream jobs and preferred to don off-beat vintage clothing.

Kyle and his roommates discovered another house for rent off of Downing Street, just a few blocks away. It was huge and had been last occupied by a branch of the then little-known Rocky Mountain School of Art and Design. The school had left remnants: blackboards adorned the walls and desks were still scattered about, as if they had left in some sort of long-term fire-drill.

Most notable was a small auditorium, perhaps it had been a ballroom back in the gold rush days. This was the house's gem. Soon Kyle would be running a secret underground venue for local and then national punk bands out of this space. Eventually known as The Classroom within exclusive circles, this auditorium also provided a consistent stage for Kyle's latest band, Zoon Politikon. This discreet location became one of the coolest places to be. In starving artist fashion, Kyle and his companions had discovered fulfillment in scarcity. The satisfaction of making something out of nothing—a lost drum set, a forgotten part of town, angst feeding the hunger of creativity and innovation.

Pat Donovan, Kyle's bandmate and author of many of their lyrics, nailed the feeling of the time in an interview with our local arts paper, *Westword*. The article read:

"Donovan believes the group's hometown has something to do with Zoon's originality. 'Denver is so small that it's an opportunity,' he says. 'Isolation has allowed it to become something different.'"

Isolation. That can happen in a crowded room when you have nothing in common with the crowd. Feelings of being outcast, misfit, *different*—we found each other by commiserating over our isolation and then created our own inclusiveness, if not becoming then *exclusive* to only those few that leaned into the glorious remoteness of this moment in time. This phenomena would start to rub off on a few more eventual icons of the city in due time.

THE PILLOW FACTORY

Ironically, even though Dad cautioned us to veer away from downtown, he was the very person who had introduced the urban parts of Denver to us in the first place. In the early 1970s we would pile into his car to head that direction because Dad had started a new venture that Kyle and I affectionately called, "The Pillow Factory."

The early 1970s television shows that had streamed across our vision when we were children boasted bright, fantastical, rainbow-colored sitcoms and variety shows that acted as a subversive antidote to the otherwise turbulent events of the Vietnam war and the human rights movements of the era.

It seemed there was a mixture of translations of postwar 1950s kitsch and hippie counterculture represented. I remember watching a tuxedoed Tony Bennet crooning a lovely ballad on *The Ed Sullivan* show, while the next performer might be the explosive mini-skirted and shimmying Tina Turner. I marveled at the magic and vibrant pinks, paisleys and jeweled sets of the *I Dream of Jeannie* show.

Sporting a peace sign on our tie-dye shirts was the norm for my brother and me. It was indeed a time period of change culturally, if not aesthetically. Dad ran with the times.

He partnered with his friend Fred to manufacture and sell contemporary home décor, which in the 1970s resembled items right out of Jeannie's bottle itself; decorative pillows in every color of the rainbow, groovy bean bag chairs, outrageously giant pillows made out of furry leopard-spotted material and chairs made with a curvy egg-like shell that went over your head like a cozy hood with radio speakers built in! It was an imaginative fantasyland to my brother and me.

The Pillow Factory, officially named Today, Inc., was not far from charming Larimer Street, where we indulged in our favorite pizza at Josephina's. It was a Depression Era building situated at the edge of the railyards, where old structures had not been kept up, either abandoned or used as warehouses.

The old Twentieth Street viaduct, stretching over the train tracks, passed at the mid-section of this building. It fascinated us that the entrance was at the second floor in order to allow access from the level of the viaduct, avoiding the underbelly, which was dark and often sheltering the homeless.

While Dad attended to paperwork and Mom must've been sweeping up bits of discarded fabric, Kyle and I discovered secret, creaky, narrow wooden staircases that led us into the upper attic areas of the building. This tippy top part had not been cleaned out from the last tenant. Rooms were stuffed with props for department store window displays. Every holiday you could imagine was represented, from festive red and green Santa and elves to brightly hued and feathery Mardi Gras Kings. The overtly grinning, mythical papier-mâché characters were randomly tossed together, as if a set for a macabre horror movie scene. The display was made less spooky by all of the comforting Colorado sunlight streaming into the tall, old windows and illuminating our youthful capers.

The bowels of the building were filled with all of the materials for making the mod furniture and accessories that Today Inc. manufactured. Sometimes we jumped and climbed on tall mountains of foam. Stepping carefully around the sewing machines, my brother and I gathered discarded pieces of the rainbow-colored and fluffy fabric that we would take home for art projects.

Years after the viaduct was torn down, transforming this area into the Ball Park District, I would enter this very building, meeting my brother to see a friend's band. As we ordered beers at the bar, he looked at me with a twinkle in his eye, "You know where we are, right?" The confused look on my face was my answer. "This is the Pillow Factory!" he exclaimed, extending his arms in symbolic possession of the building.

I was stunned but overjoyed that one of our special childhood places was still standing and remained firmly situated on our map of family places. I felt a pang of sentimentality, if not a vehement sense of ownership for this part of Denver that reached deep into the vault of my memories.

In my post-college days, the lower downtown area of Denver had changed little since the years of the Pillow Factory. It was a quiet area with pockets of the past hidden under the viaducts. The viaducts, really just grungy bridges, had been originally built in the late 1800s to aid in transport of goods over the railyards, the Platte River and Cherry Creek, but also to keep pedestrian traffic away from the train tracks.

I learned from going to the Pillow Factory to avoid going *underneath* the viaducts, but as twenty-somethings, Kyle and I were desperate to locate authentic, original places. Every so often we would discover a jewel tucked beneath one of them. Like a 3.2 bar called Rock Island where they had a toast bar in the basement and girls dancing in cages or the historic Wazee Supper Club, the second oldest bar in Denver. My adventurous brother definitely led my way to those places. He ventured under the viaducts in search of subjects for his photography. His photographs are now a preservation of those gritty places that are long gone.

The temporary status of living with my dad and his constant *USA Today* updates made me passionate about finding my own "Third Places." Not work, not home, but a place *I liked* and *chose* to hang out in. As I searched the city, I was also searching for the landscape of my soul, my identity mirrored in the city.

THE 'PEC

I met Kelly while hanging out at the bar one night at Josephina's listening to a live band. I thought I was listening to jazz, but this gal quickly schooled me and then offered to take me to a real jazz club.

El Chapultepec was located near what was considered then the edge of town for those of us brought up in the suburbs. Its location at Twentieth Street and Market was considered a northern boundary that you did not cross. With the dark vastness of the railyards to the west, this area was barely considered a "safe" part of town.

But I really wanted to go. Now I had a guide.

I picked Kelly up at her parents' house in south Denver, grabbed some cocktails-in-a-can to be thrifty and headed to that forbidden north edge of town. We parked in a dirt lot across from the post-Prohibition bar, and during buoyant conversation, downed our cocktails. Kelly assured me that someone at the bar would surely buy us drinks. Not having many occasions to dress up, we had donned what we considered our modern beatnik best: black miniskirts, fishnet stockings, oversized men's suit coats and stilettos.

It was winter and the small windows of the old bar were foggy with the breath of its patrons. The place was tiny and ancient; three old wooden booths and a petite bar hosting the ghosts of visitors like Jack Kerouac and a range of musicians from Etta James to Wynton Marsalis. The floor was an unforgettable faded red-and-white checked linoleum, dulled by the scuffs of many a shoe.

There was never a cover at The 'Pec and visitors consisted of anyone from after-theater yuppie couples to the winos from across the street. All were welcome. But frustratingly there was no dancing permitted.

We received a rousing welcome from half a dozen jazz enthusiasts, mostly suit and tied men over the age of fifty, greeting Kelly like an old friend. The band was set up at floor level at the end of the room, squeezed uncomfortably close to the ladies' room where a gal might risk getting hit in the bottom by a trombone slide.

As Kelly predicted, drinks were purchased for us with the unspoken understanding that we politely listen to the old guys' stories, which were actually quite informative. Kelly could hold her own in the conversations about different musicians. I listened intently. I wanted to learn about jazz

With Kelly's assistance, I began to "de-mystify" jazz. Like many forms of art, you can feel intimidated or resistant to participate for fear of not knowing *enough* about it. The biggest learning curve with jazz was to simply be open to it; open to its unpredictability, its storm of ideas all colliding at once, and the emotions the players evoked. It was not necessarily a code to be cracked but a collection of feelings to be embraced. Feelings that might not be able to be expressed any other way.

I was already available to jazz for the pure reason that I innately loved it. Much of it brought up sentimental feelings in me of "the good old days," a sense of history. Sometimes it reminded me of moments back at Vivian when Dad would turn up the radio, Ella Fitzgerald or Frank Sinatra crooning, and take Mom's arms in a spontaneous dance in the kitchen.

I imagined being part of the Jazz Age when people

dressed up to go out and demonstrated a certain level of manners that would elevate a moment. I loved the music's spontaneous nature that embraced "mistakes" as part of the charm and the individuality of any particular player. The wordless jazz expressions made me feel like some songs were written just for me.

As time went on, I found my own favorite tunes and players. Chet Baker and Miles Davis would narrate melancholy cloudy days for me, while the discovery of Bill Evans's mellow piano seemed to stir hidden workings of my soul. Louis Armstrong and Ella Fitzgerald simply made me smile.

One way or the other, that first trip to The 'Pec supported my navigation to those beloved Third Places as well as established a lifelong love of this nourishing and inclusive form of music.

LOOKIN' GOOD
AND GOIN' OUT

The babysitter has been booked for tonight and Mom and Dad are going out on the town! My brother and I partake in the festivity of the preparations by jumping on my parents' bed as we take in the scene.

"Going out," is an event for all of us at Vivian. It is a process indeed. Figuring out what to wear could take my mother all day, sometimes requiring a last-minute trip to the mall. Looking good is well rehearsed for Dad, as it was part of his job. He and Mom labor over their beautification rituals in order to look not just their best but *the* best.

Their bedroom becomes an overload for our young senses. Vibrant paisleys and groovy giant flowers on shiny fabrics adorn the parade of clothing that comes out of their closet. The combined fumes of Halston and Pierre Cardin colognes with Right Guard deodorant and Final Net hairspray create a toxic cloud over our heads. The hair dryer runs intermittently and their shared vanity is crowded with a colorful array of cosmetics, lotions and other products intended to beautify.

Dad's mission is singular. He proceeds in his coiffing seamlessly. In contrast to Dad, Mom tries on numerous dresses, all of which could rival the fashions of any Hollywood starlet, mostly sleeveless maxi-dresses. But Dad is critical as she goes through her closet, dresses piling up at her feet. I disagree with Dad and marvel at Mom's good looks and pretty dresses. But, oh, the trial and error that she goes through; trying on different shades of lipstick and eye shadow, teasing her hair into a fashionable bump on top of her head and spraying the hell out of it with hairspray. Kyle and I cough from the cocktail of aerosols and Dad's smoldering cigarette. I observe carefully as Mom does her make-up. My favorite is the frosty pink lipstick.

Although his grooming is well rehearsed, Dad descends the stairs far later than mother, as is his habit. Connie, our teenage neighbor, has arrived to babysit and Mom has helped us to start making popcorn. I hope to stay up late enough to watch Don Kirschner's rock concert on TV. Mom and Dad exit in a flurry that I will someday compare to my future prom nights. As I transfer to questioning Connie about her teen life of boyfriends and high school, part of my mind imagines what fine event awaits my parents, all glammed up.

Despite the fact that, as time progresses, Colorado casualness eventually usurps the need to go through such a fuss when going out, both my brother and I have inherited the need to look good. Our way consisted more of finding just the right vintage jacket or one-of-a-kind pair of shoes, curated through meticulous shopping at thrift stores and funky shops in Capitol Hill.

We cultivate our own unique styles with specific attention to random but important details. Sometimes I take something I purchase and alter it to make it fit in with my own style. Once, this consisted of cutting the tops off of a pair of beautiful, new suede boots and spray-painting them lavender. Clothing was another art form to us, the ultimate path to self-expression.

My Brother's Bar

*"A saloon was the birthplace of his voice... the
launch pad of his identity."*

—J.R. Moehringer, *The Tender Bar*

My boots are loud on the time-worn wood floors as
I scurry around trying to remember the catsup. My
anxiety at getting everyone's orders right is calmed by the
comforting smell of malt and yeast. The savory aromas of
beer brewing are akin to bread baking.

I left my last crappy waitress job with no notice because
I could tell this place was special. My co-workers exhibit
just as much sweat on their brow but way more grace.
Although they are a sarcastic bunch, I feel an electricity
in the air.

I had accidentally stumbled upon a revolution. A pinnacle moment in time that I really didn't fully understand
yet, but that followed the "make something out of nothing" philosophy. This would become my work place for a
short time, but a Third Place for many decades. It would
become an inspiration and model, if not the epicenter,
of many good things to happen in Denver. At the time,
it became a detour that influenced my path, and more
significantly, my brother's.

The beer was served authentically warm, or room

temperature, with very little carbonation, following the traditions from Europe. Your average Coors Light-swilling people did *not* like that. At first. This was a revolution in Renaissance fashion. This was the beer of monks and abbeys.

As with a lot of new trends, patrons only trickled into this former warehouse directly across from the cavernous Union Train Station and just one block from the old Pillow Factory. It was like a quiet coffee house, or someone's living room. Initially, bearded ZZ Top-looking men – home-brewers, sampled the beer like it was fine wine. They took up each pint with the discerning approach of a food critic, knowing that their approval would be appreciated by the owners of the Wynkoop, who had earned tenures from time in dark basements coaxing yeast and hops into a unique elixir.

I was getting an education I didn't know I needed. They even served the wort. Wort was the liquid extracted from the mashing of the malt before fermentation during the brewing process—basically, the base of the beer flavor before adding the alcohol. It was served hot and had little bits of the malt floating around in it. It didn't look good and from what I observed from the patrons' faces, it didn't really taste good (I never dared to try it). But here we were, at the infancy of our first craft beer phenomenon. We called it microbrewing back then as it was named in rebellion to the big breweries that held court during the twentieth century. This was cutting edge stuff! But as with many new and different things, it was considered weird and not immediately accepted by the masses.

From the moment you walked in, though, you could tell—forgive the pun—somethin' was brewin.' Denver's first microbrewery was conceived initially by John Hickenlooper and his fellow laid-off engineer friend Jerry Williams. These guys, not unlike myself in theory, were fatigued by the uninspired life of the corporate world that the 80s had commanded. The superficial glamour of the time period was quickly coming to an end, rapidly being replaced by the more down-to-earth trend that was musically narrated by the Grunge movement. The Berlin wall had come down, communism in Russia was failing and we'd soon have a Democrat for a president.

Hair got longer on men again. Clunky Doc Martens, comfortable flannel shirts and happily worn-out Levi's were donned instead of power suits and popped collars. At least in our circle, at The Wynkoop, a new way of living was spawning that valued creativity a bit more. I was in!

The Wynkoop founders were *makers* in the truest sense. Preserving the high quality, grass-roots nature of their product was top priority. Hickenlooper was a natural PR man who liked to chat and visit with customers and neighboring business owners. He established small town relationships in this area that had been dormant, sparking a genuine sense of community that became infectious.

The charming squeaks of the tall wooden double doors of the entry announced your arrival. Additional creaks in the aged wooden floors narrated your steps while you were there.

The malt and yeast used for brewing the beer engulfed the senses, embracing you in a warm, olfactory hug. That yeasty smell always invoked a cozy, welcoming feeling in me when I was there. The floor plan was open with the large, rectangular bar greeting you at the right, where eventually crowds gathered happily rubbing elbows. Large windows straight ahead looked into the brewery. Small, tall bistro tables were to the left and further left was the open kitchen where the surly line cooks created beer-infused, English fare. I was a little afraid of the cooks as they yelled at me a lot.

The employees here were different from my past restaurant jobs. My peers were either recent college grads or students on the long-term plan, tediously putting themselves through school. Like me, they were also frustrated with their situations; impatient with Denver's economy and lack of opportunities. Did any of us really want to be working in the restaurant industry? But The Wynkoop made you think about it. This idea was defying the economy by bringing a new and scrappy idea to the forefront. Yes, it was a risk, but that made it all the more attractive.

"Look alive!" a short but scrappy waitress bumps me as she trundles past, tray held high. "You're in the weeds!" she calls over her shoulder, smirking at me. She had long blond hair similar to mine and a pretty face with a pointed nose held high. For such small stature, this gal had gumption. She was younger than me too. As much as she belittled me, she also intrigued me. She was so forthright and confident. At first I hated her because she pointed out every little thing I was doing wrong. But she was funny and had a loud, high-pitched laugh. Her name was Andrea and she was the most frank, non-bullshit person I had ever met. Despite the wide gap between our personalities, she would eventually become a lifelong friend.

I did not become a great waitress, but patrons seemed to let me pass because I was friendly and enthusiastic about the food and beer. I was so green to waitressing, made a lot of mistakes, got in people's way, annoyed them, as Andrea confirmed out loud. I got a little too comfortable one night, sporting my uniform T-shirt after bleaching it and pairing it with a funky thrift store skirt instead of the required jeans. One of the managers shut that look down.

Even though everyone had a bit of an edge, came off a little mean, I appreciated the grit. That grit was reflected inside and out of the old building. There was character everywhere.

As I navigated my way around microbrew, I was finding my way around my life. Working for these beer geeks who were doing their own thing, trying out their dreams, their spirit rubbed off on me.

It took some guts to start a business where trains and the homeless dwelled in a deserted town with a bad economy. They exuded a pioneering spirit. I admired their guts, ambition and optimism to strike out on their own and take those risks.

What did I really want to do?

While making the rounds to my tables, I made mental lists about what I wanted in life: I don't *want to sit at a desk all day. I* don't *want to wear power suits and panty hose. I* do *want vacation time. I want creative freedom.* Through the lens of this invigorating experience, I began to sense some answers to my dilemma.

At the Wynkoop I became more at peace with my lack of direction. We were all striving to "figure it out." As I got to know my co-workers, I started to linger after work to quaff my shift beer or take a stroll around the corner to nearby haunts: the dark and moody Terminal Bar, or a vibrant, artsy place called City Spirit. These places became our churches, our homes away from homes... places to talk it all out, have a drink, contemplate, read or discuss and commiserate.

In a way, these situations provided an existence I had been craving—a camaraderie that provoked existential questions that we tackled together, trying to make sense of the world before deciding how we would be in it. Throughout this time period, a creative and industrious wave of people continued to give birth and sometimes rebirth to some of Denver's greatest places.

I am now keenly aware of the special places that are the "other" home for many. During those years of internal searching, I became attached to my Third Places that consoled, inspired and fed me. Perhaps that is why I have felt a profound loss as many of them disappear.

My brother and his buddy got tired of shucking oysters

at the seafood place around the corner, so I suggested he stop by the Wynkoop. Both he and his friend got jobs at the 'Koop. In a short time, Kyle went from sous chef to dessert chef to eventually the third head brewer. Although I eventually quit working at the Wynkoop to pursue my own dreams, by way of my brother, and Andrea, I continued my relationship there for years, hanging out after work to quaff my lifetime supply of "shift beer," where everybody knew my name.

THE PINK DESK

An important destination on the road trip of my life's journey was planted onto my personal landscape through my mother's penchant for giving new life to second hand furniture. Our kitchen chairs were old, repainted a cherry red and emblazoned with a patriotic eagle and crest on the backrest, fashionable around the Bicentennial year of 1976. The shelving for my brother's Hot Wheels cars and Lego collections were reclaimed from some other inevitable doom and painted a happy lemon yellow with orange trim.

And with fate sprinkling its dust of destiny, at one point Mom found a charming 1800s wooden school desk that at first glance I would not have cared for, its worn natural wood seemed plain to me. Then she worked her magic and painted it a wonderful frosty pink, just like her lipstick. From the moment it was placed in the corner of my bedroom, it became my teacher desk and symbolized my eventual life's vocation.

Carl Jung calls it concretization: an attempt to materialize our emotions and significant life events, as if we could take them, handle them like a block of clay and form them into the images that they emote for others to view, consider or ponder. But the endeavor is mostly for ourselves—like a scrapbook of our lives or...a memoir. *Some* objects *do* matter and can serve as documentation, proof of a life, of our psyche, and the substantial experiences that have been chiseled into our spirit to make our lives unique works of art. That frosty pink desk has evolved to represent a concretization of my teaching career.

Before we had video games and twenty-four-hour cartoons, I sat at that desk immersed in a methodical silence. That solitude permitted me the luxury, if not necessity, to ponder. It still amazes me how the serendipitous placement of a particular item in a room; a warm lamp or a shelf to house favorite books, can transform an environment and sometimes provoke new behavior. An item placed, just so. Changing destiny. A magical renovation.

I put ink to paper in my first diary while sitting at that desk, setting in stone a proclivity to write the rest of my life. I calculated my future age for the year 2000 on my first calculator. And most evident, I practiced my first skills as a teacher as I led either a mute classroom of dolls and stuffed animals or my less willing younger brother and exasperated friends in dittoed lessons and simple math assignments. Teaching was the only type of job that I consistently and actively practiced as a child.

In many ways nature dictates who we are from the moment we emerge from the womb. We are loud or quiet, considerate or self-absorbed. Some of us have the aptitude to be doctors or aggressive sales people, while others might prefer a life as a store clerk or waiter. I, myself, was a first child, a rule follower who naturally led my brother around in an instructional manner as many in similar birth order may do.

Then there is the phenomenon of nurture, where we have the opportunity to allow our environment and our social interactions to affect us. Perhaps if my mom had not added that antique desk to the décor of my room, at that particular time, I may not have been as positively provoked to practice being a teacher...

Teetering upon the possible fate of waiting tables for the duration of my twenties, I sped down the highway of a teaching career with optimism, fed and inspired by the grounded feeling that I had finally figured out this part of my life. I know now that it was a destiny cultivated by both the nature I was born with and the nurture provided during my early years of life.

I figured that teaching was the perfect career for someone who was creative. I could exercise that creativity with the children. It was a great job for an active outdoorsy Coloradoan, who liked to get home before dark to go for a run or mountain bike ride after work. I also know now that it was an avenue that empowered me to pay homage to my own childhood, to sort of reconcile it by helping to make other children's early years as happy as possible. I sought to bear witness and give validity to that fleeting but vital time period. Teaching eventually gave me a productive outlet for the positive memories of Vivian that I'd held close and dear. The pervasive melancholy of that loss was turned into a positive energy for what would become a passionate vocation for me.

Teaching was not my father's dream for me. I knew that. My decision was influenced in spite of his ideas for me, and also by the lack of jobs during that time. The soul-stealing, authoritative and stifling environs of corporate life as it presented itself to me in the 1980s would never be my fate. Although I may appear reserved or quiet at times, I had an independent and very liberal streak. I wanted more control over my occupation and, as corny as it sounded in that time period, I wanted to make some sort of difference in the world—ideals that originated from all those years observing Mom go to meetings and that made my father roll his eyes. I abhorred the idea of having to kiss the feet of whoever stood on the next rung of some inevitable corporate ladder.

My days at my frosty pink desk were calling to me!

While still working at the Wynkoop nights and weekends, I took on a day job in a preschool to get experience while I juggled my certification classes around the corner at Auraria Campus. It was an almost impossible and dizzying schedule, but I was elated. I became a good student again, sitting at the front of the class, raising my hand constantly. I found I was much more invested than I ever had been during my undergrad years because I knew what the result of my schooling would be and I was paying for it myself. I finally became truly connected to my education, a revelation that would continue to drive and inspire me as a teacher for years to come. One should be connected to their education.

Something crackled in me—a spark igniting a fire that was fueled by the feeling that I had found a calling. As I progressed in my classes I discovered a program called the Colorado Preschool Project. This job gave me solid roots in more thoroughly understanding child development as I also studied it in class. The Colorado Preschool Project groomed its teachers to scout for learning challenges in the preschoolers and offer them the necessary support in order to set the stage for overall school success. The awareness of the need to administer early intervention during these years became a responsibility I have taken on ever since.

I proceeded in my education like I already knew how to teach, channeling those days at the pink desk. As I read and learned and gained experience at the preschool, I brazenly challenged my instructors when I disagreed with their assertions about how children learn. Perhaps the neural pathway nurtured by my mother, with her flash cards so early on, gave me the conviction to speak up.

I did feel like a dormant switch in my brain was flipped back on. I had instincts. Everything I read made sense and seemed to work together, from Hugh Mearns' *Creative Power* of the 1920s honoring students' role in making decisions to Eleanor Duckworth's 1970s treatise acknowledging children's "having of wonderful ideas."

Progressive education reform movements during the 1980s emphasized the importance of early learning and recommended best practices for tackling this unique time of child development. Developmentally Appropriate Practice established that children under the age of eight learn differently and that curriculum and teaching methods should reflect this.

THE RED SCHOOLHOUSE

A friend of a friend connected me with a possible internship at a small but mighty independent school on the east side of town, housed in yet another 1800s massive, old, red-brick block of a building that had once held one of Denver's first kindergartens.

I met the head of Stanley British Primary School in her cozy, sunlit upstairs office. She rocked in her white rocking chair, expressing to a small group of listeners in her English accent that children here learned *by doing* and that the morning was a precious time where they made choices.

The aesthetics of this old building seemed to complement the activities of the children. Walking through the school, we were privy to what "Choice Time" was all about. Groups of children constructed magnificent block buildings in a spacious hallway adjacent to a grand staircase that reached up to lofty ceilings. Classrooms were buzzing while students chose from a magnificent variety of colorful materials in bins: knitting, watercolors, board games. Some children lay on their stomachs on the carpet, settled into squares of sunlight coming through the tall windows, and worked peacefully and independently in their math books. By choice.

As I took in all of this colorful, happy, engaged activity, I felt like I was Dorothy opening the door to Munchkinland. It overwhelmed and inspired me. I was rediscovering what school could be. I wanted to be a child again and go to school here, but maybe I could teach here instead.

As the teachers described their methods, I realized that they were happy and intellectually fed by their methodology. Teaching here seemed to enable them to have more positive effects over the environment than I had observed in other quiet and colorless classrooms. There was the overarching philosophy at Stanley, but each classroom was unique. The staff and parents had such positive things to say, not just about teaching the children, but in many ways about living life robustly. As I had experienced in the pioneering spirit of the Wynkoop, I was literally on the cusp of a progressive movement here. I was enchanted.

Listening to the headmaster explain the value of the morning's choices, I learned that the curriculum evolved from the children's endeavors, ensuring their interest in the topic. By learning *how* to make choices at this stage in development, they were learning valuable life lessons. In a traditional classroom, our choices are made for us most of the time. *How will we learn to make choices when we grow up in adult life, if we never get to practice?* she posed.

Soon, after demonstrating some of my newly acquired teaching skills, I was thrilled to get an internship there, paying in the fall of 1989 a modest $17,500. But Stanley British Primary School would become the inauguration of a teaching career that would forever, from the moment I stepped into that historic building, cause me to challenge the traditional and champion the progressive.

Miss Jill:
A Day in the Life

They enter through a heavy door held open for them, descend ten steps, often counting as they go. There is a long, carpeted hallway—they run! A set of gentle bells announces their entry into my classroom.

"Hi, Miss Jill! What are we doing today?"

Thus begins my day with a collection of "mini-people." Low in stature, but mighty in personality, these youngsters charge through the activities I have set around our colorful room, furnished completely at their scale. They dump and fill, paint and draw, play act and build.

My own thoughts and sense of self are temporarily obliterated by their every need. I am "on hold" while we play. At the same time, whatever void is created by this pause in who *I am,* they simultaneously fill me up with their enthusiastic discovery of just about everything. I have opened up their world, helped them to discover the joy of interacting with others, of squishing playdough, of embracing a story or song. Simple, but not.

Perhaps that is why I am exhausted by the time they climb back up the stairs through the heavy door and into their mamas' arms.

My mission is to accommodate the three main aspects of their development: physical, cognitive and emotional—the whole child. An observer might argue that there is only one facet of development at this stage— emotion! These tiny, chubby-cheeked people are filled with a constantly revolving spectrum of happy, sad or mad. But they learn fast. Their brains will never grow as much as they grow now.

There are many definitions of "teacher." The old-fashioned idea being that we "mold brains," by a method of stuffing information into them, usually as the children sit and listen. I do not believe this is the best way. How bold of humans to think that they can "mold" someone else's brain. The best way to grow a brain is to do it through experiences, when we are young and with the support of caring and knowledgeable adults.

I bend, squat and contort myself into the little chairs so I can look them in the face, these cherubic souls whose parents have entrusted me to guide them through their very first school experience. The moms and dads and nannies learn too.

"Miss Jill, Josh will only eat peanut butter sandwiches, what do I do?"

"Miss Jill, how do I know when my daughter is too sick to come to school?"

"Do they need their coats today?"

In this way, the mommies are just as exhausting as their children. But I respond with empathy and information as I secretly dare to envision becoming a mother myself one day. I might suggest the power of a carefully placed "No," and reassure that a child won't be malnourished if they only eat peanut butter for a while, and yes, if your daughter's congestion is beyond her control, it would be better to keep her at home. Please bring your child's coat, we go outside every day.

Mothers can beat themselves up about not being perfect. Or of working away from home at the same time. Or of not understanding why they might feel alone or lonely sometimes as stay-at-home moms. Some feel like it's a betrayal to not just embrace and cherish that time. I want to comfort them, to give them hugs too, because there are a myriad of emotions in constant flux when you so vehemently love these tiny people.

I ring the bell, "Meeting Time!" We joyfully sing a song. We have, mostly, learned how to sit for a story, especially if it is a good one, like, "Where is the Green Sheep?" Before our meeting is over, I introduce an activity related to the story, such as making our own Green Sheep out of playdough. Somehow, I have piqued their interest to the point that they are all wiggly with anticipation, ready to race to the big round table where we do our group projects. I dismiss them. "Please walk!" I call out, as some of them run to the table.

We make our playdough together, each child getting a turn to add an ingredient. "Miss Jill, am I going to get a turn?!" several children inevitably ask. "Yes, you will, don't worry." When all the ingredients are dumped into the big bowl, we take turns stirring, counting together with each revolution of the big spoon.

Sometimes I marvel at how a simple activity can engage them for so long. But I remind myself how new everything is to them. And, quite often, I am reminded of my own childhood, where my brother and I could busy ourselves all day with our fort-building and pretend play.

This is a truly precious time, I quietly observe as they pound, push and mold their portions of the dough. When it seems they might be finished, I pull out my small plastic animal collection and, again, we are ecstatic. "I want the elephant!" "No, I want the elephant!" I offer a camel or penguin and remind them that they can trade later, modeling how to ask our friend if we can have their animal when they are finished with it.

We clean up. We wash our hands thoroughly, "Billy, did you use soap? Rub your hands together!" We eat a snack. I try to teach them how to have a conversation or "conservation" as one boy says, as we eat. I model how to ask each other questions.

We clean up again. Use the potty. They gather their belongings into backpacks and run back down the hallway and up the steps, counting them all, one through ten, "Good job!" I release them onto the playground, where my role is different—entirely a safety monitor. But their bodies are strong, they are growing fast and again amaze me with what they can do. They swing, climb, and run.

Smiling moms are at the gate after their brief respite from their charges. Some children race to their mom, one lingers and says, "I don't wanna go!" with fake tears. I say, "We're closing the playground till tomorrow!" Mom gives me an appreciative look. "Goodbye Miss Jill, see you tomorrow!"

Rooms With A View

Navigating the rickety stairs outside this Denver Square, I enter the top floor apartment of an old house in Capitol Hill. *This is it,* I say to myself, my new home. No more crappy, carpeted studio apartments with windows so secure that you couldn't see out of them. There were wonderful old wood floors and delicate floral wallpaper adorning the kitchen walls. I had two gorgeous large windows, crowned with beautiful stained glass pink flowers, looking down on the neighborhood like a pair of eyes. This place had character and for only one hundred dollars more than I had been paying for my one room place. I had four rooms, one to spare for an office/studio. I couldn't believe it!

By now I knew this neighborhood well, as my old place was just a block away. It is one of my favorite parts of Capitol Hill, within a block of "Queen Soopers," the affectionately renamed grocery store in the heart of what was mostly a gay neighborhood and adjacent to many well-kept 1800s mansions near Cheeseman Park. There was also a diner and a laundromat in this small business district that remained an affordable area because of the still unchanged economy, now moving into the 1990s.

Although I had no friends in this neighborhood, my brother was still just a few blocks away. I loved walking the crooked flagstone sidewalks canopied by mature trees and taking in the sights of the grand architecture of Denver's first houses.

I worked hard on decorating my first real apartment. I had learned from Mom how to take thrift store finds and create my "shabby chic" look with paint and elbow grease. The finishing touch was to display my beloved collection of favorite books on a homemade shelf. Back then I didn't have much. I used the armoire that once held my school clothes as a new house for my small television and stereo. My futon was now just a couch since I had a real bedroom. In my "office" I begin to use my typewriter and dwell in the freedom of space and possibility as I write poetry and create random artworks with paint, clay and other media.

But something was missing.

JANE THE DOG

A soft, black clump of fur obscures the windshield. A smack of drippy dog saliva strikes my cheek over and over again. I have a dog now. My first dog of my own. I had been thinking of getting a dog ever since acquiring this top-floor-of-a-house, not-a-studio, first home, which had the bonus of shared yard space, which immediately gave me permission to look for that *first dog*.

I headed to the dog shelter that Saturday morning just to "browse." I was lonely and I should have known that a person such as myself cannot just *browse* dogs. You fall in love and take one home. Which is what ended up happening.

As I walked the hallways of stalls that held the sad or mad-looking lost pets, I summed up what I wanted in a dog. I thought I wanted a big dog, somewhat intimidating to strangers, protective. A girl dog. A somehow *cool* dog, of course.

Then there was Jane.

Jane was a medium-sized, fluffy, black lab mix. She sat in the corner of her kennel forlorn, head drooping. The description read "six-month-old," so I thought she might get bigger and it was good that she was young so I could "train" her and she otherwise looked "cool." But she also looked sad. I continued to jot down the numbers of the other kennels of the dogs I wanted to visit with that morning.

Jane, as I soon named her, was brought to me first. The staff had given her a bath right before they brought her to me. The dog that entered was nothing like the one I had seen through the glass in the kennel. She pounced into the visiting room, still-wet from her bath and frisky. She leapt up to my lap in a full-on happy doggie hug. "Ok... I'll take her!" I had to! She was already mine. And she was already Jane. I don't remember how or why, but I loved that name and she was my first baby.

From then on, for the next seventeen years, through the progression of boyfriends, cities and dwellings, and eventually that real, human baby, Jane was my longest-standing companion. With Jane as my guide, we walked or ran the streets of Capitol Hill together, getting to know every crack in the sidewalk, every other dog barking through wrought iron fences. We walked daily among the display of rundown Victorians, the ugly 60s apartment buildings and the turn of the century mansions. This was both Molly Brown's and Jack Kerouac's former territory and I loved the gritty, lost luxe that spoke to me at every block. We claimed our neighborhood by walking through it every day, gaining familiarity. Yet I loved being surprised by some detail we might've missed before, like a random gargoyle staring down at us or a horse post still remaining near the sidewalk.

I took my longest solo hike, twelve miles in one day, with Jane tethered to my pack. She made me feel brave when a hiker coming the opposite way notified me of a bear on the trail ahead. I think Jane scared the bear away.

Jane climbed 14ers with me, running ahead and then back to check on me. By the time we'd reach the top she probably had climbed two 14ers worth! Despite being petite, she was extremely strong and full of endurance. If she was thirsty, she merely drank water out of my hands. I remember cross country skiing with her. I had a pretty strong kick and glide, but with Jane harnessed to me, we went fast!

Jane became my constant companion, my new best friend, my someone-to-take-care-of in my formerly solo existence. A source of unconditional love. I had my house, my first job and, finally, a bit of a sense of family. She was a terrific watch dog and barely needed to be on the leash as she would never stray far from me. As a matter of fact, it was tough for me to travel anywhere without her, as she would somehow escape, a black dot getting bigger and bigger in the rearview mirror.

Nature as Stress Management

*"Wilderness is not a luxury but a necessity of the
human spirit, and as vital to our lives as water
and good bread."*

—Edward Abbey

When I am climbing over rocks on my mountain bike,
I feel like my neural pathways are visible. Biking
has been my therapy since before I knew what that was.
If you could *see* my thoughts as I ride, I imagine that they
would appear as a fluid banner of words flowing out of my
head behind me. They are released like a balloon leaving
a child's hand, renewing me, emptying out my busy brain
for the next batch of issues, thoughts, ideas.

Sometimes, back at Vivian, I would descend those pea
green carpeted stairs in the very early morning to find the
front door wide open, framing my dad, in that yellow terry
cloth robe, holding a cup of coffee and staring, mesmer-
ized, upon the eastern horizon.

As soon as I peeked out, I would see what had gar-
nered his attention: the sunrise. The striking colors of
the day dawning, evolving through the filigreed bare
winter branches of the cottonwoods. I would stand next

to him in quiet reverence of the moment, bonded in our joint appreciation.

Maybe because Dad had grown up in a rural environment, he was the one usually pointing out the glories, as well as the perils of nature to me. He has never stopped being amazed at Colorado and how sunny and beautiful it is. He has that ever-present perspective of having grown up in a much harsher, sterile landscape.

Mom helped us to create bird feeders in front of the kitchen windows, jump-starting my knowledge of our native birds. Red-winged blackbirds would swoop at you if you stepped too close to their nesting grounds. Swallows soared above me in happy, swirly flight. Magpies and Starlings took a stance in the ponderosa pines just outside my window, waking me too early in the summer with their annoying squawks.

Because Vivian overlooked a large reservoir, we had all sorts of wildlife nearby. Sometimes a fox would run through the yard, an orange streak against our green grass.

Dad taught me my directions when I was young and they are forever linked to Vivian. I had asked why, on one side of the yard, the snow had not yet melted. "Well, that's the north side of the house," he informed me, "it gets all the shade." From there, he reminded me that west was easy, as that is where the mountains sit. East is opposite west and the direction of downtown. South is opposite the north side of the house where the sun dwells. All my life, when someone is confused with directions, all I have to do is to visualize Vivian.

I spent many a summer traipsing through the foothills on hikes with the family or my Girl Scout troop. I have fond memories of sitting at campfires singing songs, making s'mores and gazing at the heavens to learn my constellations. The onset of autumn is an event in Colorado, where, if you are lucky, you will ascend into the mountains to witness the Aspens displaying their changing leaves like drops of gold fallen from heaven, decorating the deep green forests. In the winter I was lucky to spend excursions frolicking in deep, fluffy snow. At home Kyle and I were on our bikes with a neighborhood gang whenever possible, riding around the block.

It is an understatement to say that if you are from Colorado you are "outdoorsy." The outdoors beckon every day. The barefooted, coatless child that I was grew up to be a runner, climber, mountain biker and skier. Outside was a necessity. A cloudy day can send me into a depression, they are so rare.

As I entered the responsibilities of adulthood, stress would sometimes invade my world. A first-year teacher has a lot to learn. I had done so well at school and had such a passion that I may have been a little over confident. I was caught off-guard by the criticisms I received from my director about how to communicate with the parents, which indeed had not been taught in school *or* during my internship—an important aspect of teaching.

Those initial struggles, as humiliating as some of them had been, were crucial to my learning and future success. Especially working in a private school, parents hovered. Just because I knew a method was a fantastic way to teach did not mean the parents knew it. I began to learn the art of public relations with those parents and was able to finally use some of the skills I had learned in college. I headed off questions by writing thorough weekly letters that cited professional research to back up my methods. I became my own marketing professional and it worked!

But on the truly stressful days, the outdoors was my antidote. I could easily run five miles after work, now with Jane keeping me company. Getting my heart rate up outdoors helped to loosen the tightened muscles and relieve the unproductive thoughts that the adjustment of "first-year teacher" provoked. I required the outdoors for survival and suffered if I could not get out.

The Forest Ranger

Arnica, Showy Daisy, Indian Paintbrush....the vibrant colors of the fleeting yet abundant wild flowers of the high elevation forest animate my footfalls as I follow John. Although I had not been looking for love, I met John in class while we were both pursuing our teaching certificates. A handsome blond, his chiseled features were often shyly obscured with wire-rim glasses and sometimes his grandfather's old hat. Baggy khakis and flannel shirts with a white T-shirt underneath were his daily uniform.

Despite his good looks and sweet demeanor, in the beginning I never considered he was "my type." He was *nice* and *intelligent!* My high school boyfriend had been a unique-looking guy with an equally unique non-conformist attitude and witty sense of humor. After him, I had stints dating musicians and self-proclaimed artists or poets, anyone who seemed a bit alternative or off-kilter. That's the type of guy I pictured myself with, a guy my father wouldn't like. As it turned out, not surprisingly, everyone would end up loving John.

Not immediately apparent because of his choice of baggy clothing, John was also very fit and an accomplished outdoorsman. The wilderness was a piece of me that had been neglected during this hectic, city-dwelling, paying-for-college-by-myself/waiting tables time period. John was not fit from going to a gym, he was fit from a life of seriously recreating in the outdoors. He and his buddies did not brag about how many beers they could drink in one night, but how far they backpacked in a day or the fact that they did that hike carrying a fifty-pound log over their heads to repair a trail. Harkening back to my childhood explorations, running barefoot in the empty fields and riding my bike everywhere, I soon embraced this lifestyle as we spent time together.

Reawakening my wildness...

John only attended school part year because the rest of the time he worked as a forest ranger in Northwestern Colorado in the Medicine Bow National Forest. Soon I was visiting him at Stub Creek Ranger Station where we backpacked all through the unbelievably beautiful Rawah Wilderness Area.

With everything on our backs—tent, sleeping bag, food, water, rain gear, extra clothing and sometimes a stove—we hiked deep into the forest. We were far, far away from everything. I have intense memories of surviving strong storms above timberline when the only thing between us and the lightning was the neoprene of our lightweight tent. Looking back and knowing more now, it might have been safer to camp back down at a lower elevation, but otherwise John was extremely knowledgeable and well prepared.

Hiking through the lodgepole pines I beheld stunning plant life I hadn't seen in the foothills, like the fabled Amanita Muscaria, the red-topped, white polka-dotted (and poisonous!) mushroom that I previously thought existed only in fairy tales. Elephant Heads are an unusual bloom whose tiny purple individual "heads" look like the trunks of elephants. I experienced child-like delight when observing miniature strawberries growing along the trail, which John informed me serve as a yummy treat for the deer (and sometimes the bears).

In my previous mountain-dwelling experiences, the largest animals I had the chance to spot on hikes were deer, elk and sometimes antelope. Moose were not something that had lived in the Colorado Rockies for some time. But they were prevalent now because of a reintroduction of just twelve moose in southern Wyoming in 1987, released just miles from Stub Creek.

This was about 1990 and the elusive moose had thrived and were abundant in the area. Catching sight of a moose was a rare thrill and I was intrigued at the prospect of seeing such a large and prehistoric-looking creature. Sometimes we would intentionally go looking for them, often quietly sitting on a ridge where willow bushes surrounded a creek below, binoculars in hand.

But we never saw a moose when we were intentionally looking for one. Then one day we were approaching a trailhead and heard some shuffling behind a gathering of trees. John wordlessly motioned for me to look through the dense leaves. Not twenty feet from us stood a sow moose and her calf. We were amazingly and a little dangerously close. We watched with cautious glee.

Then a pair of humongous antlers shredded through the branches to reveal a stern-looking and large bull just behind the mother and her child. I almost screamed at the sight, knowing that the adults together would be protective of the calf. John wanted to continue to watch as I headed to our car. Once we were inside his Jeep, the trio emerged and allowed us to observe them further. It was quite rare to see the male hanging out with just one female and a calf. A memorable moment, but we did the right thing by getting back into the car. Moose can be known to charge when irritated.

John and I also mountain biked together before it was a popular sport. We rode many ungroomed trails without shocks on our bikes. One Memorial Weekend we headed out to the Canyonlands in Utah. It was a great time to go as the high desert was just warming up, but spring was still alive in the form of many blooming cacti. I was enchanted by the red rock and dirt juxtaposed with the deep green of the flora.

I cataloged at least seven different shades of red represented in the surrounding geography—from a pinkish rose to a deep maroon. Contrasted above these intense reds was the cerulean sky, proudly displayed so spaciously. The blue was so striking I felt like I could reach out and grab a hunk of it. The open expanse of sky in this area enables fascinating cloud observations. The clouds were equally magnificent, of the cleanest white and in constant motion, contorting into shapes that seemed to be imitating the mighty rocks around us.

I wrote in my journal one morning that, *If you look carefully, you can see everything here.* I would get up early and just gaze. If I was really observant, I would locate a small dwelling tucked into a rock wall, camouflaged in its use of rocks the same shade as the mountain. Ancient Pueblo dwellings. I swear one dusky evening, I saw the silhouette of a Pueblo Indian leaping between cliffs, his hair and the fringe of his moccasins flying out gracefully behind him. I had never been quite so enthralled by a natural setting. It is indeed special.

Poetic lines from Edward Abbey's *Desert Solitaire* reverberated in my mind. We camped among the pictographs and those rock homes of the ancient Pueblo and were fortunate to have a river nearby for freshening up. During the cool early morning hours we rode the slick rock trails reaching up to the endless blue sky with views a dizzying hundreds of feet down the canyon. There the Green and Colorado Rivers converged, one a muddy green, the other a muddy orange, into one brownish river. These colossal rocks framing out the river made me think of ancient, weather-worn castles. What a gorgeous, unique landscape in its stark simplicity. It was like a lost city that also reminded me of the ocean floor.

By allowing these wild places to affect me, and add to who I was going to be, I naturally became more of a conservationist. John taught me about old growth forests, which I had yet to see. He chastised me for using paper towels instead of cloth towels and insisted that children under my supervision had to use both sides of the paper. I willingly gave up driving my car in favor of biking to work.

In the winter I learned to ski without a resort. No chairlift this time, just my muscles, and indeed they were getting strong. For my twenty-sixth birthday John gifted me a pristine pair of Swedish wooden skis that had been made in the year I was born but had never once been used. They were beautiful, and I would soon find that with just the right type of wax on the bottom, I could hang with most people climbing up the mountain with their new skis.

I was reminded of this time later in life while reading about how Ernest Hemingway with his first wife Hadley had spent lovely winters high up in the Austrian village of Schruns, where they too skied without a chairlift, using seal skins to get up steep hills and deep snow, earning every little bit of the downhill they would enjoy. Hemingway mourns in *A Moveable Feast* the eventual commercialization of skiing with chairlifts spoiling all the fun, making it "too terribly easy to get up the mountain."

During these adventures, it was usually just the two of us. John also taught me to rock climb, an activity I had never imagined doing. John was my teacher. He was a patient teacher, but sometimes I got frustrated. In the end, whether I had actually wanted to learn how to rock climb or camp above timberline or ski without edges, I tried the sport to hang out with John. But, without really realizing it, I soon became proficient, strong and independent in most of these activities, just by running around outside and having fun.

HARD TO FALL

I was not only falling for John, but I fell hard for his family too. They were the stuff of *old Denver*. His four sisters were debutantes. They had all attended the nearby and well-regarded East High School. They still ate dinner as a family at a grand old table in a mint green dining room. Mostly, when I was visiting, I felt like I went back in time. Their grand old house breathed history from its ornate details, vintage wallpaper and timeless furnishings. His mom always wore dresses, Dad always a tie. But they were not stiff or aloof. They were a warm and welcoming clan who always expressed real interest and concern for me.

Although it had been almost ten years since my parents' split, it seemed John's family knew I was in need of such a clan. Both of my parents often chose to travel with their new significant others during Thanksgiving and Easter, so I cherished those holidays at John's family's house. Because there were five siblings and Gramma also attended, it was a festive group. In many ways, I could not see myself ever wanting or needing to be anywhere else except protected within the walls and loving hugs of this household. It was probably one of the first times I thought I might really marry someone.

I was caught off guard by the lure of this possibility. Could *I* get married and have my own family? Dare I consider this? As a child playing house with my friends, this idea had been an assumed proposition, an expectation, even: get married, buy a house, have some babies, live happily ever after, right?

But clearly I had seen an end to *happily ever after* and I rarely entertained that possibility. To be tempted by the potential comfort and security of a lifelong partner scared me. *What if it doesn't work out?* As much as the core of my being wanted that life, to resurrect my own Vivian, I was equally prepared to quickly exit upon the first signs of rejection.

And it was slowly becoming clear that John was not ready for this type of commitment. Although I know he cared for me, deep down he was a loner. You might think that an only boy with four girl siblings would be especially in tune with a female's need for emotional availability and communication. But John was the classic strong and silent type. His parents had given him a large room to himself as a boy, on the third floor of the house, a sweet effort to symbolically make up for being the only boy in the family. I think he spent a lot of time on his own in that room as a child, sequestered away from his sisters, preferring quiet and solitude.

While John's hushed demeanor could be charming, when I really wanted to talk about the future of our relationship, his silence was frustrating. Despite his loving family home, we still had our own apartments, which kept things casual at a time when I inevitably felt pressure from my close friends who had rings on their fingers. As John continued to keep me at arm's length, I became more and more needy and insecure about our relationship.

What compounded the situation was his gig as a forest ranger. He would be up there for almost half the year. He called, but the call was long distance then, and actually cost extra money. We wrote letters and I would of course visit as much as possible. Sometimes he would be called away to work on a forest fire and I wouldn't hear from him for weeks. Even though I respected John's choice to serve as a forest ranger, his long absences, silence about our future and my growing insecurity grew during our third year together. If this schedule was going to continue indefinitely, then I was going to find a way to curate adventures of my own when he was gone.

SIGNIFICANT INTERRUPTION;
MONTANA

L ooking down I see the comforting and familiar rhythm
of my feet alternating against the pavement as I climb
my bike up a deserted highway near the Montana-Can-
ada border. After an interminable three-day train ride, I
am relieved to be on my bike. My bike, a steadfast friend,
accompanying me on adventures.

This adventure is the most ambitious I have tackled on
my own, and had it not been for John, I might never have
been able to do it. But now I am riding in spite of him.
Our relationship, I'd realized on the train ride, was in a
frustrating state of limbo.

So here I am climbing a hill on my bike in Montana
with a bunch of strangers.

This is a 300-mile, ten-day, bike-packing trip through
Glacier National Park.

After researching affordable options, I enthusiastically
chose to take the train to my destination. I boarded the
almost empty car, reserving two seats for myself and all
my gear. I brought with me all of the books and resources
to plan curriculums for the next school year as well as my
journal to productively pass the time.

The scenery, as we chugged along the rails into the
mountains, unspooled like a nature film presented through

the ample window. I was transfixed by these initial views, which offered such a different perspective than from a car. Trains often follow unique paths, engineered based on the grade of the land.

Unfortunately, those paths can take longer and the view out the window became less engaging after a few hours. When we stopped, although the train would never get completely full, I had to be protective of my seats. I also learned to avoid eye contact with at least one particular gentleman who kept inviting me to join him in the bar car. Each time he walked by his gaze lingered longer and his gait became sloppier.

After many frustrating delays, I was reminded of trips down to Union Station with Mom to wait for Gramma to arrive from Omaha on the train. It was always late. So much for the charm of riding the rails.

As the novelty of the journey wore off and I devoured all of my reading materials, I resorted to dissecting my life to pieces.

What was I even doing? Was I capable of bike riding all this way? Would I get anything out of this, other than perhaps humiliation?

When I emerged from the stagnant hovel of the train two days later, I must have looked like a mole squinting in the sunlight. But the gorgeous surroundings of Whitefish, Montana, immediately rejuvenated me.

I had researched the area and packed meticulously. I was going to be in grizzly country here. This would not be a trip with sag wagons to support us, everything would be carted on our bikes: extra clothing, pots, pans, food, tent, etc. We were road riding, but all I had was my hefty mountain bike. When I saw that the rest of group had lighter road bikes, my confidence again wavered.

The only other woman in the group was not friendly, and we would soon learn, gravely out of shape. The rest of the eight participants were all men, most about my parents' age and seeming to be in the throes of mid-life crises. The last two guys, my age, from New York City, seemed rather crass in their predictable East Coast, out-spoken ways and a bit full of themselves. Wonderful.

Once we got going though, I was emboldened by remarks from some of the fatherly older guys, impressed with how strong I was on my heavier bike. I began to impress myself too. I hadn't realized how fit I had become in the last few years. John and his friends were *uber* fit, so I always felt like the amateur around them. But I was killing it on the climbs so far and sustained good endurance.

It felt good to exert my muscles, to sweat and feel competent. Exercise of any kind has always been therapeutic for me. Riding my bike within this beautiful national park was exhilarating.

We were often engulfed by the huge spruces of the forest walling us in on either side of the road. Other times we rode on the flatter outskirts of the mountain range, on quiet highways. Although we biked as a group, the thin margins of the roads dictated that we ride single file, so we were each essentially alone for the duration of each day. I ended up purchasing a small mirror for my helmet in order to get a heads up when semi-trucks approached me from behind, the strong vacuum they created as they passed threatening to send me flying.

We biked through small logging towns where all the pick-up trucks brandished shotguns hanging in their back windows. Sometimes we would take a break at one of the lone bars situated at the edge of the highway, just to refill our water. We'd chat with toothless characters who spent their days nursing beers. One day we had to ride through a herd of cows that had wandered onto the highway.

Each night we gathered to cook dinner. The campsites were so much easier than backpacking in the wilderness.

There were actually bathrooms and running water. Weather on the entire trip was sunny, warm and beautiful.

Our campsites were often adjacent to one of the aqua blue glacial lakes at the base of a towering mountain. Instead of taking a shower I would sometimes take a quick swim in these ice-cold but replenishing waters.

I was soon released from dwelling on my relationship. I enjoyed being happily physical in the picturesque surroundings. My problems, compared to some of the older men, seemed ridiculous. I had a lot of life ahead of me and I was young and strong.

I scolded myself for having been so down in the mouth. This adventure was boosting me in ways I hadn't predicted. Despite my previous impressions about them, I ended up spending a lot of my time with the two New Yorkers. They were refreshingly different from Colorado guys with their fun accents and ways of talking and joking. One of them, actually a Brooklyn Assistant District Attorney, would break into a Sinatra song at unexpected moments. They flirted with me and complimented me on my strength during the ride. I don't know if I had ever felt strong, smart and pretty all at the same time. It was nice. And what's an adventure if you don't get to know people from other places?

One night we shared a six pack, lying on our backs half inside my bigger tent to keep warm, and watched for shooting stars. It almost felt like Girl Scout camp again, except with cute boys. In the darkness we each told our stories. Or parts of them. I did not confess my boyfriend troubles, wanting to stay positive. Before the conversation became too serious, we were gifted with the performance of an orange comet, sizzling across the sky, directly over our heads. We were astonished.

I understood later in life that my proclivity to flee in the face of conflict, as in the form of this trip, would become a pattern for me. Leaving before a hurt set in was my solution for dealing with my life's struggles when they plateaued. There was indeed a fight or flight element going on that I eventually realized was deeply influenced by the unaddressed feelings of abandonment from my parents during their divorce.

This abandonment, that went undefined for years, follows me well into my adulthood, resurrecting my inner child during tough times and defying any growth I might have thought I had gained. One of many therapists poses the theory that I choose romantic partners who are "unavailable." Yet, even with this pointed out, I continued to subconsciously *prefer* men who are unavailable. Maybe I wanted to keep things temporary, never gaining the type of intimacy that would risk a deep hurt when things didn't work out. In the meantime, fleeing became my vehicle for healing myself. It certainly kept things interesting.

Now I'm on the pinnacle of our ride, the Going to the Sun Road, an arduous mountain pass. When I reach the top I feel like a new woman. It seems like the entire continent is flared before me, ripe with new opportunities. I have realized my value with a group of strangers and surprised myself with my physical abilities. I feel worthy. Somehow back in Denver I didn't. One way or the other, I see with clarity that I no longer feel valued in my relationship. It is as evident as the spiny mountain road I just conquered. I had needed more than an adventure. I need a big change in my life.

By the time I board the train for home, I am prepared to *purposefully* do some thinking, provoking further changes in hopes of feeling happier about my life.

BUTTERFLY

I was restless. I wanted something to change. And as much as I cared for John, I knew deep down that simply forcing the idea of marriage on him was not necessarily the answer to that. Additionally, at twenty-seven, I still felt naive. So many people I interacted with were much more seasoned, traveled, and overall much more experienced at life than I was. I realized marriage was not the answer for me either if I hoped to become worldlier, but I did crave a deeper connection in a relationship.

I loved my well-earned Capitol Hill apartment and having Jane the dog there. I had a *good* job, however low paying, and I knew I was getting exceptional teaching experience. I had a nice, smart, good-looking boyfriend, but who was often absent and hesitant to share himself.

We were in our third year together and I was getting an itch. Was this how I was going to proceed in life? Give up, break up, move on? Was this the lasting result of my parents' split? I didn't know yet. But the urge to flee rather than fight further for my relationship with John was palpable.

I sought an *otherness*. An escape from my comfortable-enough environment into an unknown territory in order to grow, learn more about myself, become something better.

The Woman
in the Photo

The woman in the photo is me, it seems, just a few minutes ago, but also a very long time ago. She took this photo herself with her 35mm set on the timer. She took it in black-and-white in an attempt to be artistic but also to be taken more seriously at a time when it seemed no one did.

During this recent past she worked hard to put herself through school to become a teacher. She looks younger than she is and her big smile, blond hair and agreeable demeanor seem to misrepresent her intelligence. She *is* young, and a bit naïve, but her goals and intentions are passionate and intentional. She craves respect.

She does not feel either respected *or* pretty right now.

Her smile was made beautiful by braces that she tolerated during a delicate time of her early teens, when she also wore glasses. Boys jeered at her in the hallways of junior high, calling her names, *dog* and *four-eyes* being the lighter of the words thrown her way. She was quiet, but smart, almost always earning straight A's. She was a good kid.

The ugly duckling she believed she was grew up. The braces came off and her mom got her contact lenses—not so ugly anymore. But inside she was still that shy nerd who liked to get a stack of books from the library and sequester herself in her room to read and write in her diary and dream. Part of her is still the quiet girl with braces and glasses. She has accumulated achievements, yet never learned how to stand up for herself.

This *first house*, where the picture was taken, was her first *house of her own* where she could again have the type of solitude, security and peace that she had in her childhood bedroom. This photo reveals some of her insides. She is contemplative. She is not always smiling within. She winces remembering a male co-worker who once scoffed that she "must be happy all the time!" That ignorant comment has resonated with her. She wants you to see her complexity in this black-and-white photo. Her angst, pain and yearning that she cannot yet define, but that has recently required her to leave this *first home of her own*.

She has cleaned out this home, just now. There is nothing left in the bedroom but the dresser that was there when she moved in. That dresser that she had reclaimed by polishing the wood and adding the pretty porcelain drawer pulls with pink flowers. She wishes she could take it with her.

She had felt so lucky to find this top-floor-of-an-old-house apartment in her favorite part of the neighborhood where she could walk to the store when she didn't have a car. It had wood floors! She had always wanted wood floors that represented the history of a house. The big plate glass windows were a bonus. She loved to peer at the street below, just like she had at Vivian.

She has read and written alone in this bedroom in the summers while her "beloved" has left her again for the third year in a row to wander for six months in the high country, guarding the forest. He has his own solitude there at tree line. She misses him and is often confused that he keeps leaving without her, but she accepts this sadness and collects her loneliness, her dog at her side.

In the summer she'd kept the window open and often heard her neighbors enjoying beers on their front porch. Their laughter drifted up to her and made her feel more alone. Sometimes they invited her, but they were older, had lived more, were rougher around the edges. She didn't know what to say to them. Yet she yearned for a tribe of her own. People she could confide this sadness, try to understand better. Solitude or the protection of a group? For now she chooses solitude.

As that third summer progressed, she ended up having too many nights like this. She thought, *enough for now*, to no specific conclusion. The isolation caused a simmering of realizations. Inside she starts to explode with frustration. The "beloved" rarely calls. She feels abandoned. She goes out, dates other men, cheats on the "beloved." Then ultimately feels horrible about it.

She sits one more time in her now empty adored first house. It is time to leave. No more waiting, watching, thinking, listening to others outside the window. It is time for a fresh map. For something else to happen. She is not sure what it is, but it is urgent. Yes.

She has her self. She has her dog. She will take parts of this *first home* with her in her mind, through her journals scribbled in late at night. She takes one more look out the window.

CALIFORNIA

My alarm sounds, and as if still dreaming, my eyes land on a Dr. Seuss-looking tree outside my window. "Where am I?" With a jump in my heart that is both excitement and panic I remember: "I moved. I really moved. I am not in Colorado anymore and that tree is a palm tree. I am one block away from the beach in Southern California."

I write in my journal:

> *In striving to do the right things, we often forget to listen to ourselves. As scary as it sounded and as lonely as it can be, moving away from everything I know and love was a necessary thing I needed to do. I feel a wonderful ownership of my life, a clean slate that has enabled me to think and see things more clearly.*

Everyone balked at my decision to do this. Dad pulled out every negative statistic about California. My friends scoffed at the absurdity of the idea. My mom, perhaps in defiance of Dad's negativity, attempted support that was cloaked in a weird sad-angry demeanor, ripe with all of our unreconciled baggage.

California, along with Texas, has always been Colorado's symbolic nemesis. It was hardest to tell my brother, who had been making raspberry beer the day I came into the brewery. "Denver's just getting great now, why would you want to leave?" Heavy crocodile tears brimmed his lower eyelids. His white shirt, stained from the raspberries, almost looked like it was smeared with blood. That was a tough moment for me. I felt like I was abandoning him.

During the first weeks in this strange land, I wake in the middle of the night calling, "Daddy!" In this recurring dream I am a toddler having been sent to my room by my mother who was navigating her pregnancy with my brother. I stand at my window in the dream holding the gauzy-white curtains like a giant handkerchief as I cry and call out for Daddy to come home and rescue me.

During my first three months I became indoctrinated into the realities of natural disasters in this region. First, through a horrible fire that blows through Laguna's most expensive neighborhood and narrowly avoids our humble rental. Not long after that event, I awake in the middle of the night when it seems my bookshelf has turned to rubber and something was moving my bed around. "Teri! Is this an earthquake?!" I yelled to my roommate, sleeping in the other room. "Yes!" she called back. The epicenter of this 6.7 point earthquake was up the coast in Los Angeles, the Northridge Quake. We experienced little damage, but I don't ever remember feeling so environmentally vulnerable before.

I have "acquaintances" who were introduced to me by Colorado friends of friends who live in the vicinity. One night, I take a walk with a guy who knew a friend of mine from high school. I meet him at Dana Point, the next town down the Pacific Coast Highway. Fall is in full swing now, yet I enjoy the warm breeze as I walk barefoot down the pier.

I am aware that I am missing my first winter. It feels strange and wrong at the same time that it feels good to still be wearing lighter clothing. I share with this guy that I am enjoying the warm winds. They remind me of the Chinook we experience in Colorado in early fall, a week-long stretch of delightfully warm winds that briefly tame the falling autumn temperatures just before the leaves fall and winter sets in. I remember when these winds would arrive at Vivian. Mom taught me the name of them and ever after we would smile and look knowingly at each other and say, "Yep, the Chinooks have arrived."

But these winds, my companion tells me, are the Santa Anas, also called "devil winds," as the prevailing legend goes. Rather than a pleasant phenomenon these winds arrive carrying bad omens along their breath. They can reach high speeds causing wind damage and fire danger. Not the same kind of wind...

We sit on the beach. There is a crescent moon colored red, partially from the dust and pollution disturbed from the winds, but it is nevertheless pretty and creates a crimson glow as dusk sets in. Three Latino boys frolic between the surf and a beached log near us.

I hear them call each other "the mens." They adopt the log as their pretend boat and are deeply engrossed in their play, their jumping and leaping little bodies make artful silhouettes against the pastel-hued background of sky.

I glance at my companion realizing his tangled locks are the same color as the moon. We quietly watch the boys in unison. Our observation breaks the spell of their game and they suddenly spy Jane, who I, of course, bring everywhere that dogs are allowed. Jane is cute and everyone likes to pet her.

The boys slowly approach, the oldest whispering cautionary words in the others' ears. They seem to be brothers, in sizes small, medium and large. The youngest looks at me with imploring eyes as he reaches out towards Jane. I nod in approval and his little fingertips gently graze the fringe of her ears. The oldest boy cradles the top of his brother's head and lovingly pets his hair. And then they are off, giggling and leaping, back into their boat.

The sun has set with a chill in the air. We walk back. I will never see that guy again.

THE AUSSIE

"How's she going, eh? Care for a beer?" I love his accent. My new boyfriend.

He has emerged from the ocean, seemingly in slow motion, shaking the water out of his shoulder-length hair as he strides towards me, his surfer muscles emphasized by his snug wetsuit.

I sigh to myself with admiration for this presentation. Only every once in a while I ponder, "Do I only like him for his looks and his cool accent?"

He is Australian and we both found each other as "outsiders" in this fabled place. We have become united in our disappointments in Southern California. We resent that our naiveté was influenced by how the West Coast was portrayed to us as children, duped by the make-believe lifestyle reflected on film—endless pristine landscapes and fun-loving, open-minded attitudes.

Whether that California ever existed, neither of us has been able to pin it down. The beaches have been abused and the landscapes beyond have been overdeveloped. Instead of the refreshing progressive atmosphere I had hoped for, this Orange County piece of coast is disappointingly conservative.

"Home has better waves than this mush they call surf," The Aussie complains. Fueled by the beach blanket movies of the 1960s, he had envisioned a utopia that he now realizes is more actualized in his hometown of Perth.

Yet we have each made promises to ourselves, individually, about what this adventure is supposed to be. I stubbornly search for even a small enclave of my imagined beach life here where like-minded creative bohemian types sat huddled in the sand around a campfire, enthusiastically discussing intriguing topics.

Despite his disappointment in the surf, The Aussie realizes some of his career aspirations here, working for the environmental non-profit The Surfrider Foundation. This national organization, headquartered in San Clemente, helps to clean up the beaches and spread awareness of the rampant polluting of our oceans. A talented artist, The Aussie will soon have one of his original illustrations published in a *Rolling Stone* article about the foundation.

I had landed a job teaching kindergarten at a well-regarded private school in San Juan Capistrano, just a short drive inland. Working with children, I continue to realize, grounds me. Teaching comforts and connects me in a positive way to my own childhood and feeds into my goal of fostering a greater good in the world.

One of my charges, an adorable kindergartener named Elizabeth, arrives each morning with her long blond hair maneuvered into a top knot by her mother, giving her a mature appearance. Additionally, she often shows up to school wearing rose-colored, heart-shaped sunglasses. She is a character.

One day during quiet time in the afternoon, while most children color or do puzzles, Elizabeth chooses to watch me while I struggle to cut some cardboard for a project. She senses my frustration and begins a game with me. "Miss Jill! Would you rather cut cardboard or eat spaghetti? Would you rather cut cardboard or skin your knee?" Her game became a metaphor for my current life choices; to myself I was saying, "Miss Jill, do you want to stay in California or go back to Denver?"

At the end of my school day, driving back out to the apartment I share with a native Californian, I get a fun surprise when I glimpse the blue foreverness of the ocean. A perfect line on the horizon that contrasts in my mind with my previous indigenous rocky western view. Whatever struggles I may experience at any given time, natural landscapes rejuvenate me. Jane and I run down to the beach each day to dip our feet into the Pacific and watch the sun set like a big round flame dousing into the fluid vista.

As much as I missed my mountains, sitting in the sand and staring out at the ocean becomes an irreplaceable practice that provides me with a daily spiritual cleansing. There will be times in my future where I will feel a pull back to the water. A need for that cleansing, the expanse of the water transferring my gaze through my mind into a necessary nothingness.

I like my co-workers, mostly older women, but it is clear that my ways of teaching seem foreign when compared to their unquestioned commitment to traditional methods. The surrounding conservatism, fed by the money in the area, makes me feel like I'm back in the 80s. I'd hoped I would take part in a collective vision embracing my reformist views not only about education but about life. It becomes clear that just because I was on the West Coast, *this was not* an assurance of lifestyle. Oh, I still had so much to learn!

Furthermore, despite my instinct in hand-picking an apartment in Laguna Beach, I begin to realize the importance of a city center that cultivates community. I was so tangent to downtown Denver's revitalization that, even though Laguna *looked* like it had a center, I could not locate its heart.

Laguna is definitely unique and pretty. It is situated at the western edge of Laguna Canyon which cuts through the San Joaquin Hills and a wonderfully preserved open space, rare so close to the coast. Laguna Canyon is inhabited by a granola collection of artist-types, which was part of the attraction for me. The main beach, however petite, is a focal point along the Pacific Coast Highway that leads downhill from the north into town. The coastal face of the hills host adorable bungalows with open-shuttered windows facing the ocean and looking over the bijou town.

I am seeking a connection to this place. I am looking for those Third Places that helped to fuel my life in Denver. But the tourism that supports most establishments makes it hard to be considered as someone other than a visitor. If there is a "center" where locals gather, it remains a secret to me.

I continue to be either amazed or disappointed as I explore the beach areas. I learn about "Taco Tuesday." Those fresh fish tacos are wonderful. I watch in awe as surfers coast and careen over the waves, the feminist in me wonders why I do not see one woman out in the water.

I am further irked to learn of beach culture fashion—for women, the less clothing the better it seems. Tight shorts that graze the edge of the buttocks, and "half shirts," are some of the uniforms of the beach babes. Teeny tiny bikinis holding in fake boobs seem to be a requirement for the girls who greet their wetsuit-clad surfer boyfriends as they emerge, aloof, from the water.

To add to the *alternative universe* feeling of these new surroundings, the longer I live here, I end up defying my own ethics. After meeting The Aussie, and becoming one of those girlfriends waiting for her surfer boyfriend, I indulge a bit in the fashion, in attempts to fit in. It eventually becomes my new norm, but every time I visit home I am reminded of how demeaning and patriarchal it is to expect the women to sit on display, scantily clad on the beach, while the men are out there having fun in the water!

My frustrations inevitably rub off on The Aussie. Things are intense and passionate with him, never easy. To further compound the situation, he is in the States on a visa and admits that falling in love, because of his temporary status, was not on his agenda. We were both clearly engaging as a couple on the defensive that the other might bolt back to their respective home.

But it is too late, we are in a relationship, and frankly, he is the only friend I have here. Each time The Aussie travels back to Australia to see his family, we embrace at the airport like we might not see each other again. Customs does not always let you come and go more than a couple of times on one visa. We spend every day together. Whenever he is Down Under, I throw myself into my teaching.

———

"Miss Jill! Your teaching methods are amazing! Frannie has started to write stories at home," a mother shares with me one day. Despite the agonies associated with being a newcomer, my hard work is finally paying off and parents are seeing the fruits of my labor with their children.

"Whole language" is an approach I use to teach young children the beginnings of reading and writing. This approach allows me to connect all forms of literacy to help make the task of reading and writing more accessible to the children.

Rather than spending lots of time on the phonics worksheets the school provided that separated language into parts, I use children's literature to inspire the kindergarteners to make up their own stories. Depending on the skills they arrive with, I instruct my students to create a drawing and then begin the writing process by labeling their picture. This method empowers the children as I coach them to sound out words on their own. They may begin this process by writing words using only the strongest consonants, such as writing *cat* as CT. But as the semester progresses I help them listen for and add the vowels to their words.

Some children possess enough letter sounds that they began writing full-page stories at home as well as at school. This is an impressive event for most parents and I received many accolades.

While the staff seems to resent my use of alternative methods, the parents are so pleased that they begin to solicit the administration to permit me to keep their children in class through second grade, initiating a multi-age class like I had taught at Stanley.

These parents are go-getters and when the administration balks at their suggestion, they suggest that I start my own school with them. This is an incredible opportunity for me as well as a huge boost to my ego. The only problem is that I don't know how long I want to live in California to be able to commit to such an endeavor. The pressure I experience from the parents begins to trickle into my relationship with The Aussie, forcing me to figure out my future sooner rather than later.

FLIGHT

I am going home. I am on a payphone in LAX asking Andrea to pick me up at the airport in Denver. "What? You can't just leave! Don't you have work tomorrow? Jill, it's too expensive to get a flight at the last minute..."

"I'm coming," I reply. "Can you pick me up at two?"

My ears are still ringing with the panic from The Aussie's words. As soon as he was out the door I just got in my car and drove up to Los Angeles. I was shaking the whole drive.

The way things have been going I don't blame him for breaking up with me. However, I don't know *anyone* else here. I have been unhappy, and he has been the only thing keeping me in California. But damn him for doing it this way. I have no one to turn to for comfort.

So I am going home.

Andrea picks me up. "Where's your luggage?"

"Luggage?"

Ever the reliable and resourceful friend, she takes me to a discount clothing store to pick up some underwear and shirts. "Toothbrush?" she asks, holding one up with a bit of a smirk. I can always count on her for levity.

She then drives me to the Skyline, a dive bar situated amid the train tracks where a steady stream of friends appear. All seem happy to see me. Ah, home. It is Sunday and we sit on the dilapidated wood deck, soaking up the blinding sun. They have a Sunday Special—"All You Can Drink Beer for $5,"—just what the doctor ordered. But we know our limits and later as Andrea drives me west, uphill towards my mom's house, the Front Range appears.

I am reminded of driving back from visiting my grandparents in Omaha, all four of us stuffed into Dad's car. It is an arduously boring drive through the eastern plains. At the state line, the classic sign announces, "Welcome to Colorful Colorado!" I remember our impatience at getting home. "Are we almost there?" Kyle would ask to Dad's frustration every five minutes. Mom would respond, "Keep a lookout for the mountains." And slowly, eventually, that blue wall capped with white would begin to materialize getting bigger, taller and more amazing as the miles passed through the front windshield. "Yay! Almost home!"

And I never tire of it. Seeing those mountains. I get the same thrill, the same warmth in my chest. My place. My home.

As Andrea drives, we are presented with an outrageously brilliant Technicolor sunset. "Welcome back," it says to me. The moody light reflects a gentle pink on our faces, as if saying, "Just come home, Jill!" I am indeed homesick. I start to cry as I confess the failure of my California experiment. "Australia is a long way away," she offers, "maybe it's all for the best if he is set on going back there."

"Yeah." I am comforted by the sun setting over my familiar mountains, putting on this beautiful light show.

And even though Mom and I don't consistently get along, even though she lives in a house that hasn't yet felt like home, I am happy to see her. I still need her.

When I walk in the door she is flabbergasted. We embrace and I tell her all my troubles at her kitchen table. This helps her home feel a bit more like *home* to me at that moment.

When I return to California, The Aussie and I reconcile.

It had shocked him that I ran back to Colorado so easily. But despite our strong feelings for one another, we know this is an impossible situation. When I lie next to him, we hold each other in futility, just looking at each other with love but lots of sadness.

We go right back to fighting more than getting along. This is a challenging situation for anyone. To give us credit, we try many scenarios. He travels back to Denver with me several times and my family loves him, but he can not bear the idea of being so far from the ocean. As he reminisces about Perth, I can't help but respond with similar feelings about Denver, and this causes us to resent each other. We have completely different life-maps on opposite sides of the globe and our places of origin are more like necessary limbs we can't live without.

At work I have inadvertently isolated myself from my peers with my insistence on using alternative teaching methods that are, basically, in direct opposition to how everyone else at the school teaches. An eventual "badge of courage" I will bear for the rest of my life, that one person in a group who must fight that *good fight* no matter what. I am stubborn and refuse to give into the cookie-cutter curriculums that the school provides. Although the parents are on board with my methods, my co-workers become increasingly frustrated with me for rocking the boat.

Because I am so dedicated to teaching in reformist ways, I am blind to the perspectives of others. To me, they are simply wrong and unenlightened. My experiences at that school in California will be the first template in my journey as *educational rebel*. As time marches on, I will cultivate more digestible ways of sharing my ideals in a school environment, learning an artful version of compromise. But until then, I simply make everyone miserable in my assertions of right and wrong.

Losing out both personally and professionally, I sit on

that beautiful beach almost every day, while The Aussie surfs, feeling deeply depressed and conflicted. To an outside observer, this may look like a nonproblem. I have a good job in a beautiful part of America and a handsome boyfriend. My surroundings are gorgeous, but there is little connection or substance for me here, which, for me, is like starving. It all feels shallow, as if we're on some fake movie set.

At the culmination of two years, in August 1995, we are both headed back to our respective homes with the Band-Aid of an idea that I will try to get a teacher exchange job in Perth. I actually work hard to explore that idea, but my gut instinct (to flee, again) resists moving *that* far away. By the time I pack up my car, trusty Jane in the backseat ready to return to Denver, our relationship has taken many tolls. When The Aussie walks up the hill toward his own apartment after saying goodbye, I watch him until I can't see him anymore. I know with a heavy heart that it is probably the last time I will *ever* see him.

Reentry: No Place Like Home

The scene at the brewery relieved and warmed my heart. Nothing had changed—even the collection of mostly male regulars sitting on stools they have claimed as their own, discussing the same minutiae that they had deemed vital two years ago. The Wynkoop, still my living room away from home, contained many beloved essences of Denver: beer, that soothing smell of malt and yeast, quaffed by unpretentious, faded jean-clad patrons and encapsulated in a gold rush era building that exuded as much warmth inside as the strong sentinel sun streaming through the six-foot-tall windows.

I was home for good. California was not for me, but living there had helped me to continue to define what *was* for me. By experiencing environments where I did not feel embraced or connected, I was distilling the features of place that called to my soul. I had searched for the heartbeat of the West Coast but wherever it might have been, it must regularly float out on the waves of the Pacific.

Here I beheld anew the brilliant blue cloudless sky showcasing that dazzling yellow sun that was brighter than at the beach, somewhat mythical here at 5,280 feet elevation. I could experience the productive hum of downtown Denver, that underdog spirit, or escape to my foothills for an amazing silence that provoked contemplation.

As I reacquainted myself with my home, pumping my bike up the rocky trails of South Table Mesa, I rechristened myself in my hard-earned sweat that reminded me that part of my self is here in the dirt, the thin air, the beer and the people I love. And I had missed it. I had missed myself.

Good Limbo

Once at a teacher's conference the lecturer drew two lines on the white board—one, a simple straight line, and the other a complicated scribble. He told us that the scribble was more reflective of true learning. We rarely master subjects, but rather we ideally question them, test them and ponder them, get to know them. Learning is the epitome of struggle. I was indeed learning and I was going to give myself a break for not having my life in a perfect straight line.

Through my successes and failures in California I learned that I was a good teacher and that my best asset with the children was my passion, openness and creativity. With The Aussie, I mostly learned that I needed to proceed slowly in any future relationships. I needed to take more time to get to know a person before I put all of my eggs in his basket.

I remember getting home from trips with my parents and being so grateful to be back at Vivian, my launch pad, my home base. I didn't have Vivian anymore, but I did have my city. And, like me, my city was growing.

Hickenlooper, our Wynkoop founder, had had such success in Denver that he was running for mayor. Our new baseball stadium was being constructed just blocks from the brewery, reactivating the long-abandoned but historic buildings in the lower downtown area. As I walked from the 'Koop to the Wazee Supper Club down the street with my brother, I could feel an industrious spark in the air.

After all of the intensity of my relationship and job in California at the age of thirty I took a gradual transition back to my life in Denver. I wanted to work on my passions. I rented a cute little house from my mom and her husband on the west side of town. Instead of diving right back into another teaching job I decided to substitute teach while working on some projects. I was going to be my own compass.

The Refrigerator
Door Gallery

While substitute teaching, I became reawakened to the art that the younger children were producing in their free time. It was unabashed and raw, and at times, I thought, existential. Sometimes I would stay after school to continue art projects with the students who were interested, usually children in grades kindergarten through second grade.

Through research I endeavored to further validate the spontaneous renderings of this time of life, early childhood, and the drawings children produced. I stumbled upon art historian Jonathon Fineberg's book, *The Innocent Eye: Children's Art and the Modern Artist*, which paralleled great modern art works by Miro, Klee, Picasso and Kandinsky with the children's art that had influenced them.

It was stunning to see the similarities, if not the flat-out plagiarism that these artists committed with children's works as their muses. I called my project The Refrigerator Door Gallery, which became a roving display of children's art that adorned the walls of local businesses. I participated in my own First Fridays, advertising these exhibits in the local entertainment weekly

My after-school art projects with the children also became "framing sessions," where we would paint and decorate thrift store frames for the art. The result was a vivid display that honored the unfettered creativity and innocence of early childhood paired with quotes from Fineberg's book, providing The Refrigerator Door Gallery the validity required to qualify as an "authentic" art exhibit.

I never made money during this endeavor, yet my events drew good crowds and my name was associated with a novel idea. The Refrigerator Door Gallery was a genuine passion project for me, signaling my ability to put ideas into action.

ELITCH'S

1980

It seems the last time I had a close group of friends, I was still securely situated under Vivian's roof. I was in junior high and we were marching over the July-heated pavement, pocked with rounds of discarded Juicy Fruit and Bubble Yum. The scent in the air was pungent and sugary. We had crumpled dollar bills in our pockets, earned from mowing lawns and babysitting to help pay for the greasy snacks that enticed our group as we entered the grounds of Elitch Gardens Amusement Park.

They blasted our music, served our food and provided just enough unsupervised thrills. Ah, those precious days when summer seemed to last a year. Long lines at the roller coaster could shorten in the blink of an eye when you were holding hands with your first love.

This was an urban part of town where we mingled with all different shades and backgrounds of fellow teens, united in a similar rite of passage; to experience the best summer of our lives, free in the sun before the serious responsibility of "future."

When you are fifteen, your friends are vital to your existence. In adult terms, we hadn't been friends that long, but we had that conviviality of shared experiences, inhabiting the same vicinity of one another. I somehow already had an innate awareness of the fragility of these moments. We have to grow up some day and all this fun might go away.

But we had this last experience, at Elitch's, carefree and joy-filled. Our parents trusted us, dropped us off, knowing we would find their cars after the park closes. But until then, we savored every moment, every ride, every stolen kiss and greasy French fry until the sun was replaced by Christmas-like lights, illuminating the rides as if they were our special rocket ships, ready to take us to hopeful destinies.

JAY AND AMY
AND JOANNE AND KERRY

The pain and embarrassment I felt after leaving California was dissipating as I basked in the rediscovery and comfort of Denver. Things were indeed "getting great" as Kyle had predicted. There was just-enough growth happening at that time to attract a steady flow of young people from all over the country who were eager to explore Colorado.

My new pack of friends dove into our city with gusto. "This new martini bar on Fifteenth looks kind of cool," Jay, our unofficial but charismatic group leader, suggested. At this point in time, I had many options on a Friday night, and I rolled my eyes internally at Jay's suggestion; I avoided "new" places, especially with a name like Blue Martini. The very sound of it demonstrates an attempt to fancify, and thus threaten, the authenticity of my town.

"I think I'm going to check out a couple of galleries first," I responded, "Maybe I'll catch up with you guys later." Where did my confidence come from to head out on a Friday night by myself? And why don't I want to date my new friend Jay? He's super cute and smart. Had I finally grown up? Did I finally know myself well enough that I can say no to things I instinctively didn't want to do, even with people I really liked?

Apparently, yes! I will meet up with this new group of friends later in the evening. They realized the new bar sucks and followed me over to an established joint, The Terminal Bar, where, at times, Tom Waits has sat anonymously brooding at the dark bar, composing lyrics in his head and where Jack Kerouac visited so many times that his elbows eventually wore down the varnish on the bar. Such a better place!

Jay, Amy, Joanne and Kerry were a refreshing gaggle of young people who'd recently moved to our rapidly changing town. They "collected" me into their group one night while visiting another of my sacred haunts, The Cruise Room. Our secret Cowtown was starting to get discovered and Lower Downtown (which will soon be shortened to LoDo) now ranked as a hotspot. I had become their accidental ambassador to Denver.

My brother was now Head Brewer at the Wynkoop and somewhat of a public figure, as Denver had become the center of the microbrewing business. In addition to creating new beer recipes for the brewery, Kyle had been traveling around the country to help other breweries get their start. The Wynkoop helped establish The Brewers Guild, supporting new breweries in navigating municipal red tape. They also led the way when Denver hosted the annual Great American Beer Festival. In many ways, I had clout all over town just because I'm "Kyle's Sister."

The Wynkoop was my base of operation. To the chagrin of the managers, I occasionally received personal phone calls at the bar when friends couldn't reach me at home. But it's not like I didn't bring in business. A night on the town would always begin there.

After I met my new friends, I realized I had not felt tight to a group of people since that summer in 1980, going to Elitch's with my junior high school crew. This new group wanted to find out all about Denver and embraced my tenure. My new friends, just a bit younger than I, were employed in successful corporate jobs, but instead of critiquing my rebelliously cultivated boho persona, they embraced me.

It was a magical couple of years. I knew people wherever we went. Additionally, I was engaging in projects that were creative. This made me happy. I was finally being myself. Not inhibited by a societal requirement or my dad's criticism or a badly chosen relationship. I had paid some dues and I knew more of what I desired in life.

My new friends were intelligent, ambitious and extremely excited about recreating and socializing in Colorado. They were fun, and most evident to me, happy. I immediately had a group of people to go to concerts with, ski with and overall just hang out with. When not meeting at the Wynkoop, we would congregate on the big porch of Jay's house in Washington Park, where we could walk to the bars and restaurants. Many a silly night was launched from Jay's porch.

Denver was fresh to me as I socialized with this group around town. We would travel four or five to a car up to the mountains on weekends. As my group donned their new snow pants and clicked into the latest in ski or snowboard technology, I would show up in the ski pants I'd had since high school and click into my old Rossignols. They teased me at the age of my equipment, but I would redeem myself as I artfully navigated the bumps down the slopes.

This group, originating from as far away as Atlanta and Chicago, were some of the most fun, interesting and genuine people I have ever known. They were a lively, supportive group, who had the sense to prioritize fun and happiness in their lives.

Mom and Dad

I had sort of broken Dad's heart with my decision to move to California. He'd done all he could to paint an unsavory picture of the place before I left, and now that I was back I realized he'd been right about a lot of it. He was indeed glad to have me back and Kyle and I resumed our periodic treks out to his house for the occasional Bronco game cookout or off-day divorce-holiday, like July fifth or December twenty-third.

While we did have moments of joy, bordering on closeness, Mom and I were still a bit aloof with one another. There had been little progress in reconciling our differences since high school when I expressed my defiance towards her decisions. We were both busy women who rarely took opportunities to spend time alone together. Issues were swept conveniently under rugs and our relationship was strained because of the pretense. As far as conveying feelings, mine were too intense to dig up at this juncture and I was finally feeling peaceful and grounded in my own life to risk bringing up the past.

I kept my memories of Vivian at bay, as they could tease me into a funk. I was full-on into my own life, my journey having motored down roads far from our old cul-de-sac. But breaking up a family was not as cut and dried as breaking up with a boyfriend. When I broke up with boyfriends I never saw them again. It was a done, finished deal and I would move on with a vengeance.

A family lingers, with all its little broken pieces, scattered here and there, occasionally tripping me up. No glue. A family with no connectedness is almost more frustrating than no family at all. There were so many separate compartments. Kyle had lived with Mom and her husband for a time, so he was closer to them. He had a distant and strained relationship with Dad. I, of course, had my roller coaster relationship with Mom and a co-dependent relationship with Dad. I mostly felt like family with Kyle. We had our shared experiences.

In the meantime I was working hard on being happy with myself and my choices. A boyfriend was not on the agenda and having my new friends was a great distraction.

North Denver

A bell rings cheerily as you enter this cozy spot at the intersection of Thirty-Second and Lowell. This is a "Wynkoop neighborhood" chosen for its community feel and proximity to lower downtown, where many of my friends from the brewery bought their first houses, including my brother. This was formerly Denver's Italian neighborhood with ornate mason work decorating many of the post-war homes and ample venues serving spaghetti and pizza.

I had still been dwelling in Capitol Hill, but after patronizing the coffee house Common Grounds in this area of North Denver called The Highlands uphill from downtown Denver, I ached to live there. Soon I was working nights at the cafe as a barista, that little bell on the door signaling the entrance of one of the many local regulars who I began to know by name and what they ordered.

It was a wonderfully bustling place, full of cheerful conversation and familiar greetings between patrons. A real neighborhood place. Even though I was working two jobs, I couldn't wait to get to the coffee house at night. There was local art revolving on the walls and second-hand furniture was placed on the coffee-stained carpet and books were everywhere. It smelled deliciously of coffee and pastries all the time.

I soon left Capitol Hill, but there were few apartments

in The Highlands, so I found myself moving into a classic old Denver Square at Twenty-Third and Lowell with two other Wynkoop employees. I had two rooms to myself upstairs, one for my bedroom, the other for an office. Each room had a big window facing south towards Twenty-Third that let in the bright sunshine. Jane had a big backyard to play in and soon made best friends with my roommate's cat.

Having mostly lived alone, I was surprised that I didn't mind having roommates. Soon we were all converging together late at night after our shifts, cooking meals together. I loved it. But it wouldn't take me long to rock my own boat again.

THE RED PLUS SIGN

The plus sign turned as red as a diaper rash almost immediately, way before the required three minutes were up. The bit of weight I had gained I had mistakenly chalked up to eating too many scones while working at Common Grounds. The man-child in my life was sitting on the edge of the bathtub, unpeeling an orange as calmly as if he had hours to await the result. After I told him, his reaction was subdued, smoldered by too much marijuana and interrupted with a cigarette, blowing the smoke out the window. My rule was "no smoking *in* the house." I was about to get much more strict about that.

I simply didn't think I could get pregnant. I'd had close calls, but surely if I were a fertile woman, I would have gotten pregnant by now. So when it appeared that my period was late, I met up with a dear, old buddy of mine who has two children of her own. When I described to her what I thought were some strange pre-menstrual cramps, she looked at me with a knowing and excited smile, "Jill, I think you're pregnant!" To have *her* validate this possibility brought the idea to reality for me and I felt a combination of excitement and anxiousness. The prospect of becoming a mom was in a much higher place of priority in my life than the sorry excuse for a relationship I was having with the would-be father.

GESTATION SALVATION

It was shortly after Thanksgiving. We'd celebrated in our big shared house with a bunch of friends. I thought inviting Mom over for a turkey sandwich might be a good way to tell her the news. I guess I'd never had Mom over to any place I'd ever lived—not even for lunch. So, naturally she was suspicious as to the occasion. *Is Jill moving again? Does she need to borrow money? What is it?*

When I told her, I didn't quite get the response I expected.

From her point of view I was doing this all wrong. I was unmarried, not really even *in* a relationship with the guy I had met through my roommates. I had rarely been financially stable. She gave me a hard-to-read hug and a funny smile and then she left.

When I told Dad, his response was similar. But what did they expect, I rarely did things the "traditional" way, did I?

I didn't care. This was the best thing that ever happened to me. A wish come true. And I was going to make it okay.

Excerpts from a secret journal on being pregnant:

> *When I feel you kick it makes me really happy because I get so afraid that I might be doing something wrong in my daily life. Arguing with the man-child being one of them. The disbelief that this body that I perceived as flawed, could perform*

this miracle...it has made me feel whole, fulfilled, and more purposeful than any job, relationship or creative project has ever made me feel.

The length of human gestation and the patience it requires must be some sort of God-sent training ground. A time to grow up and take stock of who you are. These months are teaching me humility and providing perspective. I realize that up until now I have been so neurotically caught up in what increasingly seems like minutia. I call it my GESTATION SALVATION.

The loneliness and self-absorption of my previous single life seems so self-indulgent now. As soon as I am showing, I am at once addressed by friends and strangers with this respect. Like being granted membership to an exclusive club. I am finally partaking in grown-up life now.

RAISING JACK

From my journal:

> *Dear Jack,*
> *The moments after you were born, when I held*
> *you in my arms, I, of course, already knew you.*
> *We'd been together for those 9 + months, but my*
> *soul already knew you. My entire being; mind,*
> *body, spirit had yearned for you. I had always,*
> *quietly and secretly, dreamed of a family. A*
> *redemptive family that might heal the wounds of*
> *Vivian. Like so many women of my generation, I*
> *had strived to locate the right partner and perfect*
> *time frame for this event. Well, fate brought you to*
> *me in its own way.*

This is a love that is so encompassing, so whole and true
that I cannot imagine anyone or anything else command-
ing an equal feeling. While this is such a solid experience,
at the same time it makes me extremely protective. Nothing will intervene on me and my boy.

I spend my unpaid pregnancy leave cuddling, feeding
and just overall marveling at you. You are perfect. Cute, of
course, but I can already tell that you are intelligent.

The day you were born, a flood of family and friends
filtered through our hospital room. For one of the first

times ever, Mom and Dad, along with their partners and my brother, were all in the same room and happy to be ogling you. Only an event as significant as you making your entrance into this world could provoke such an event!

During the labor, your father was often absent, disappearing for cigarette breaks for long stretches of time after telling me to "push harder." My mother, your Gramma, stepped up and was there for me, for us. As I struggled with the birthing process, she put cool compresses on my forehead, almost like when I was a young child, sick in bed back at Vivian. She spoke words of encouragement during the labor and helped me to gauge when I needed pain relief. I could not have gotten through it all without her help. Thanks, Mom.

And then you were here, finally. Loved ones visited and brought flowers and held you, marveled at your already plumpness and congratulated us. It was the best day ever.

DISPLACEMENT AGAIN

Eight months later, I wake on a friend's couch among a now consistent series of friends' couches where I attempt to sleep while making sure that Jack is taken care of. His father did not step up to the task of fatherhood as people had hoped. He rarely works, sitting for hours in the kitchen with that damned cigarette, mulling, loitering and simmering with such a consistent anger, confusing in its lack of source.

Whatever I say makes him angrier. He used to threaten me before Jack was born and now I cannot allow this behavior. He scares me. I am emboldened by the need to protect my son. I sleep on friends' couches. I work full time. I am the bread winner. I am fortunate to have a friend watch Jack while I figure it all out.

I have dwindled to a weight less than I ever weighed in high school. I simply don't have time to eat or make food and sometimes I am so distraught I have no appetite. My mother accuses me of being anorexic, to which I respond, "Put a plate of food in front of me and I will eat it, Mom!"

My married friends invite Jack and me over for dinners. One time I overheard my friend telling her husband to make "extra food," as she has noticed that once I am served I am voracious.

Yes, this is a struggle, which seems to be written into my life's journey and my proclivity to make certain choices.

But this time I am clear minded at what needs to happen: take care of Jack in the best way possible.

This leads to legal issues with his dad. Instead of a peaceful breakup he chooses to stalk me at work and refuses to move out of the house. It takes some time, but eventually the dust settles. Not wanting to pay child support, he will disappear.

In place of that, in place of a "typical" family, we cultivate our own wonderful life. I come to realize that owning my life choices and accepting my "mistakes" are the things that make my life full and vibrant. *And,* I have learned so much. I am a survivor.

That scribbly line that that speaker at the teacher's conference drew next to the straight line resonates in my mind. My life map is complicated. It has many coordinates. The roads are often rocky. I have written notes all over it. It is messy, but it is interesting. I began to embrace the scribbly geography of my map because it was much more fulfilling than that straight line.

CELEBRATIONS

The milestones of motherhood were able to finally, peacefully unfold after Jack's dad left. And then some of the best memories of Vivian came floating back to me. It was good and reminded me of so many traditions that had been long buried in the rubble of my parents' split. I could now resurrect some of those events with my own child, in my own way.

Christmas at Vivian was always spectacular. The smell of pine was prevalent as we gathered together to decorate the tree with those giant green and red globes. Kyle and I loved to peer into them to experience our distorted faces in the glass. The Sears catalog was presented to us as we formed in our minds what Santa might bring us. We spent days making homemade ornaments for the tree out of salt dough and cooked many varieties of Christmas cookies. There was always an advent calendar and Mom and Dad indulged us with all of the wonderful myths of the season. "Santa's watching!" would be exclaimed if we might misbehave during this time, causing us to attempt angelic attitudes.

Hot chocolate was served in front of the fire where Dad sometimes popped us some popcorn. I remember insisting he get the fire out thoroughly on Christmas Eve so that Santa could get down the chimney unscathed. We lay flat on our stomachs in front of the television, excitedly anticipating the Christmas specials, like *Rudolph the Red-Nosed Reindeer* and *Frosty the Snowman*.

Pure, selfish, but joyous anticipation was the feeling for all of those twenty-four days before the holiday. When the eve of the twenty-fifth finally came we could hardly sleep. I remember looking out the window that faced my bed, covers up to my chin and thinking I saw Santa and his sleigh flying by. Mom would read us *The Night Before Christmas* before tucking us in which really just provoked more wakefulness. It always seemed like the longest night of the year.

My brother and I would tumble down the stairs early in the morning. Mom and Dad would have done it up; it seemed as if they had somehow convinced the stars from that previous night to visit our living room with magical glitter. Underneath the tree was a true bounty of gifts for everyone and the whole room seemed to literally sparkle.

Special meals happened in our otherwise unused dining room, under the festive chandelier. I grew up coming home from school when it was my birthday week to find that Mom would have adorned the chandelier with crepe paper and balloons, placed a pretty table cloth and fixed a festive centerpiece at our Danish-Modern table in anticipation for my party. I always felt very special, loved. We embraced the advent of the celebration at hand. We savored the coming of a milestone in our lives by showering it with traditions that began days before.

And sometimes a celebration would happen *just because*. This might occur when Dad had just returned from a long trip bringing some regional foods or the weather was fantastic and we would feast on snacks on the back porch together. I always loved sitting in on Mom and Dad's conversations and plan-making.

A Fresh Start
at Stuart Street

2003

With the cheerful sound of sparrows greeting the sun just outside my window, darkness transitions to a warm rose as my eyes flutter open to the pink-painted walls of my bedroom. It's today! There is a peacefully sleeping toddler next to me so I step gingerly to avoid the floorboards that I know might creak and wake him as I head to the kitchen for coffee.

This is my house. Our house. And I revel in anticipation of what we will do today. What will be our great idea? Jack will show me.

We have our own sanctuary.

I had never had a house of my own. I had rented apartments. My parents may not have approved of *how* they acquired their grandson, but they adored him and gifted us a modest down payment. I researched what was available in my price range and drove to a little house on the edge of my treasured North Denver neighborhood. These cute houses sitting next to each other, as if old friends with a canopy of mature trees overhead, presented themselves to me like charming little gift boxes. The surprises of their unique interiors invited me to fill them up with life.

I had *real* responsibility now and I fell in love with it. I was finally the cartographer of our own lives. With Jack, my life came into focus. I had a good job implementing a new preschool at a nearby independent school and I could afford a small mortgage. The Stuart Street house was invisible from the street, hidden by a wonderfully giant blue spruce tree that would be all ours. The beige, vinyl-sided structure built in the 1920s was unremarkable, but to me it was a castle.

It had pristine pumpkin-toned wood floors hiding under the dated wall-to-wall white carpeting and a working brick fireplace. I had space for an office. After the closing I spent weekends moving in, pulling up the old carpet and painting the walls fun colors.

Without realizing it, there were bits of Vivian in this house already. The warm wood paneling and hearth reminded me of our old family room. I subconsciously painted the walls the same pea green as Vivian's omnipresent carpeting of the 1970s. I chose a mid-century decorating pallet, finding lots of choices for this theme at the thrift stores.

Soon it was home.

As Jack grew he was able to attend the school where I taught which made issues of childcare moot and I could spend more time with him as a working mom. He was my charge and my buddy. I am blessed with an easy child who is developing a charming and loving personality.

Summers and weekends are, of course, our favorite. Like back at Vivian, we sustain a relaxed approach to our days, lounging in PJ's until the outdoors might beckon or a project evolves. Jack exhibits a natural tendency to be creative. One day it's a Lego creation or a cooking project. Another, he suddenly wants to sew his own stuffed animal, and he does! I love supporting his ideas.

We visit all the museums and the zoo, just like I did

with Mom. We go on hikes in the mountains and bike rides in the neighborhood. We host sleepovers with his best friend and I cherish being able to have chances to be a fun mom who bakes cookies for everyone.

For the first time, I am able to take the good memories of my childhood at Vivian and bring them back alive for my own child. I took the old snapshots of our life there and translated them for Jack, creating our own history that I would ensure would not be forgotten. And, in a way, this brings me peace about the past.

All I needed was a family, a home. Now I have my very own. I feel like I have earned this.

And as time flows on, this fulfillment will help me forgive and reconcile with my past.

THAT LAST THING

"That last thing is what you can't get, Carlo. Nobody can get that last thing. We keep on living in hopes of catching it once and for all."

—Jack Kerouac, *On the Road*

I can still emit tears. The heart hurts a little. There is nothing like leaving your childhood home forever. Vivian Street. I went back. Thirty years later. The people who had been living there for so long got old and moved out. And there it sat all by itself. Weary for the years.

But the single paned back porch French doors were unlocked and welcomed me to enter, like arms ready with a hug after a long trip. As I entered I instantly turned back in time to about the age of seven. I heard Mom rustling in the kitchen and saw my brother sitting on the pea green shag carpeting too close to the TV. I sensed Dad upstairs in his yellow terry cloth robe smoking a cigarette, taking his time. Ghosts.

Jack Kerouac in his book *On the Road* asserts to his friend Carlo, who is questioning life in his existential manner, that he can't get that elusive thing that he wants. That Last Thing. It is unattainable, utopian, not possible! Give up. You're just not gonna get it, man.

And maybe that had been part of my struggle. All

those years, perhaps I was holding myself back in the unacceptance of my parents' fate and the loss of Vivian. Maybe I was futilely always trying to get it back, to no avail. Nothing else was going to be good enough.

And then came Jack.

That *last thing* is different in origin but same in its *intangibility* for us all. For me, now, I suppose it is some sort of colliding of all my best worlds into one, and meeting together at Vivian Street. Mom and Dad would be cooking and dancing in the kitchen. All of our dogs and cats from our collective lives would observe at our feet. Our mountain view from the kitchen window would remain unfettered so that I could show my closest friends what I was talking about.

It would be Christmas at the same time and Jack would be there both as a child and as his grown self so that he could experience it in both best ways. He would meet myself and my brother as children and we would play so famously together, best friends! Outside there would be a foot of snow, but it would be a cloudless, bluebird sunny Colorado day. My pendulum-swing-time-machine, my moveable feast. I think that is my heaven. So who knows, maybe we do get it. Someday.

EPILOGUE: ENVIRONMENTAL DISORIENTATION

A pristine piece of white paper placed in the landscape position. A swatch of blue at the top, green at the bottom, delineating the clear boundaries of sky and earth. Distinctly marking the space between is a square with a triangle on top, maybe a tree or flower next to it. A yellow circle of sun graces the upper corner. Home. These first early childhood renderings are universal, a collective starting point for the landscapes of our lives. The spot on the game board labeled "GO."

This is one of the ways we instinctively begin to internalize our environment, by putting it down on paper, translating it in our own way, and beginning the process of mental mapmaking. An important part of brain development is the ability for humans to create cognitive maps of their environments. Dating back to our caveman origins, before paper maps or GPS, our abilities to remember landscapes through visual cues in the geography of the land around us were critical to survival.

As children we naturally begin mental map-making when we are carted around in a stroller or a car. We notice familiar landmarks repeated over time with routine. This ability is said to begin maturing at age four, making our surroundings a key factor in the development of our identity.

I cherish my son's early drawings of our house. He would document details that I would have missed. Just as I internalized the distinctive characteristics of my environment at Vivian, Jack would note the slight hill of Stuart Street and the zig zag of our sidewalk. Jane the dog, by then a bit of a geriatric, had lost an eye to glaucoma. This, very significant to Jack, he drew her with one eye an "x". We might forget these details over time as we grow up. Unless one lives in a place their entire life and suddenly those landmarks have been removed.

If I did not have the stability of our life at Stuart Street, it would be much more devastating for me as I observe the loss of so many special places in Denver over the last decade. Our city has grown beyond its belt straps. It's about to bust its buttons. Developers recognized the opportunity for lucrative investments in housing the hordes of transient peoples coming here from all corners of the country, seemingly equipped with endless funds.

Historic homes are flattened to accommodate intrusively huge structures that will hold faceless dwellers who never seem to be home anyway. Josephina's was eventually purchased and divided in half to house two separate and "fancy" bars that you couldn't pay me to go to.

What happens to us, to those maps inside our minds that are mixed in with our own unique memories, when these landmarks and emblems of the past that have a firm footing in our conscious, if not the sheer make-up of parts of who we intrinsically are as individual people, what happens when these places disappear?

During the last ten years, I have painfully witnessed Denver's physical history vanish. I drive around town and not realize where I am because an entire block of historic buildings or a grove of tall spruce trees that marked the horizon are just gone. These landmarks had been tightly woven into my mental map of the city, the internal map that allowed me to never need an *actual* map.

I do not necessarily disagree with progress that is collectively beneficial to a city's residents. I have strived to get accustomed to sharing Denver with many, many new people. But if we continue to allow the demolition of swaths of historic buildings the entirety of Denver will look like it was only recently constructed during the twenty-first century.

This development, this erasure of my environment, is offensive. Age-old tenants have been pushed out by impossible increases in rent. All of the places my son and I enjoyed in our neighborhood that were part of the physical spaces of our lives, those places that were part of his young identity, in the course of just a few years are gone. As if they never existed. What about that?

I had lost Vivian; my original place of identity. I spent the first decades of my adult life attempting to fill the hole that loss left in my psyche by embracing the hand-picked Third Places I discovered while mapping out my life. Now I am losing those too.

The American painter, Andrew Wyeth, who lived and painted in the same area his entire life, once said: "*Be* in your surroundings. Breathe it. And if you're lucky you will capture it." I have honored and tried to capture many of these lost places in this book and they live on in my vivid memories.

RIP: Wazee Supper Club, El Chapultepec, Josephina's, Patsy's, Pagliacci's, The original La Loma, Muddy's Coffee House, The Bonnie Brae Tavern, The Terminal Bar, Common Grounds, Local 46, Kyle's Kitchen and so many more.

Author's Note

In writing a memoir, there are many occasions where the *accuracy* of memory comes into play. My brother and I have random disagreements about how things happened in the past, as many siblings do. With that feedback from him and a few others, my shitty first drafts contained many efforts to be accurate. But as I continued to try to write well, I realized that it wasn't completely about accuracy, but about my unique perceptions of past moments.

We all have our own interpretations about the events in our lives, this is mine.

I have shared my struggles and pain of growing up after my parents' split. It was indeed a difficult time. Taking your kids to see a therapist back then was not yet a norm and the advice my parents' were given was that, "children are resilient and they will be fine." Not so much.

My parents' divorce was difficult because we experienced a strong collective relationship as a family within the walls of the home we created together. My brother and I were wholly and intentionally loved and cared for when we were young. I have reconciled my hurts from their split through my writing and do not blame my parents. They did the best they could and I still love them both as much as I did when I was four years old. They are loving, intelligent and unique people and I am grateful for them.

As Maya Angelou said, "Won't take nothin' for my journey now."

Clarifications:

The restaurant, La Loma, mentioned in the prologue, found a new home on Broadway and they are continuing their legacy there.

In the book, I criticize my college campus, Southern California and corporate life, that's just me and my opinion. But if I had not had those experiences in different places and situations, I would never have been able to so finely tune what I required in my surroundings to curate a life that I absolutely love.

ACKNOWLEDGEMENTS

First of all, I must thank my mother who has supported all of my creative endeavors since those very first days at Vivian's kitchen table, under the stained glass light fixture. She was my first proof reader and despite the fact that she knew this book contained some harder parts of our journey as mother and daughter, she has continued to champion my efforts. Thanks, Mom.

Thank you to David and Kelly of Open Books who shed light on the fact that my story might be worth putting in print. Gratitude goes to Brad Wetzler. His memoir class and its participants gave me perspective on all the different ways a personal narrative can evolve. Denver writer, Jenny Shank, I am grateful for your *writer's commiseration* and validation that Denver is indeed an interesting place to write about. I thank Dave Sabados, publisher of *The Denver North Star* newspaper, who provides me with opportunities to write on a consistent basis as well as discounted promos in the paper.

I thank Mike's Camera, just down the road from Vivian Street, for working with my old photos to prepare that picture that eventually became the cover of the book. Special thanks to employee, Ashlie, with whom I shared one of the first exciting moments of, "this is really happening!"

Barbara Richardson was an invaluable source for helping me dig myself out of all the tenses I was using and streamlining the editing process. Brett Matarazzo of BRDG Project, thank you for your support in helping plan the first book launch in my beloved North Denver neighborhood.

To my husband Jeff for your consistent belief in all of my projects and supporting me with that "year off" to finish a book that had been six years in the making. I am truly blessed to have a life full of wonderful, loyal friends both in Denver and Salida, Colorado (my Music Family!). Thank you all for your unbridled enthusiasm, support and purchasing of pre-sale books.

And finally, although she is not around to witness the publishing of this book, my life-long friend, Teresa Lee Ward Sweeney, who always left me with the phrase, "Go out there and change the world!" Teresa, I'm trying and I think you're helping me, as you always did on earth, now in your heaven. I miss you.

Made in the USA
Monee, IL
06 November 2023